A GROUP STUDY GUIDE

Based on the Classic Best-seller by Henrietta Mears

Old Testament

WHAT THE BIBLE IS ALL ABOUT 101

GENESIS THROUGH ESTHER

A 13-WEEK BIBLE STUDY ON THE FIRST 17 BOOKS OF THE OLD TESTAMENT

Larry Keefauver, Editor

Gospel Light

9780830717958

W0010687

Gospel Light is an evangelical Christian publisher dedicated to serving the local church. We believe God's vision for Gospel Light is to provide church leaders with biblical, user-friendly materials that will help them evangelize, disciple and minister to children, youth and families.

We hope this Gospel Light resource will help you discover biblical truth for your own life and help you minister to adults. God bless you in your work.

For a free catalog from Gospel Light please contact your Christian supplier or call 1-800-4-GOSPEL.

PUBLISHING STAFF
William T. Greig, Publisher
Dr. Elmer L. Towns, Senior Consulting Publisher
Dr. Gary S. Greig, Senior Consulting Editor
Larry Keefauver, Editor
Jean Daly, Managing Editor
Pam Weston, Editorial Assistant
Kyle Duncan, Associate Publisher
Bayard Taylor, M.Div., Editor, Theological and Biblical Issues
Debi Thayer, Designer

ISBN 0-8307-1795-1
© 1996 Gospel Light Publications
All rights reserved.
Printed in U.S.A.

What the Bible Is All About is a trademark of Gospel Light.

How to Make Clean Copies from This Book

You may make copies of portions of this book with a clean conscience if:

- you (or someone in your organization) are the original purchaser;
- you are using the copies you make for a noncommercial purpose (such as teaching or promoting your ministry) within your church or organization;
- you follow the instructions provided in this book.

However, it is ILLEGAL for you to make copies if:

- you are using the material to promote, advertise or sell a product or service other than for ministry fund-raising;
- you are using the material in or on a product for sale;
- you or your organization are **not** the original purchaser of this book.

By following these guidelines you help us keep our products affordable.

Thank you,

Gospel Light

CONTENTS

To complete this course in *11 sessions* combine Sessions 5 and 6 and combine Sessions 10 and 11.

WHAT THIS COURSE IS ABOUT

God's Word is vibrant and alive, and His plan for our lives is contained between the pages of His book—the Bible. Everything we need to know about living in wholeness is contained within the pages of His Word. Yet, we sometimes forget that the Bible is more than a series of unrelated, independent books—it is a connected, all-encompassing, interwoven work that provides a panoramic view of His love and plan for us.

However, the average person knows little about the Bible. Very few have a comprehensive idea of the whole book. We need, besides a microscopic study of individual books, chapters and verses, a telescopic study of God's Word in order to better understand His plan of salvation and movement in our lives. Through this study, you and your group will be able to see the interconnection between the Old and New Testaments, between the prophets and Christ. You will also see how Jesus Christ is portrayed in each book of the Bible.

The Bible is a book of 66 books written by at least 40 authors over a period of about 1,600 years. To help us gain an accurate perspective of this monumental work, we will be using the best-selling Bible study resource *What the Bible Is All About* by Henrietta Mears. This book provides helpful summaries of each book of the Bible, helping us to see the common threads of Good News from beginning to end.

As we begin this exploration, we must keep in mind that sometimes the Bible gives a great deal of detail, while at other times there are only brief statements. However, gaining the perspective of the Bible's major events and characters provides a helpful mental map in which to locate and understand the great riches the Book contains.

"The Bible is one book, one history, one story, His story. Behind the 10,000 events stands God, the builder of history, the maker of the ages. Eternity bounds the one side, eternity bounds the other side, and time is in between: Genesis—origins, Revelation—endings, and all the way between, God is working things out. You can go down into the minutest detail everywhere and see that there is one great purpose moving through the ages: the eternal design of the Almighty God to redeem a wrecked and ruined world" (*What the Bible Is All About* by Henrietta Mears, page 20).

In this course, *What the Bible Is All About 101 Old Testament: Genesis—Esther*, group members study the book of Genesis through the book of Esther. God's workings and revelations are discovered while seeing how Jesus Christ is portrayed in each of these books of the Bible.

THIS GROUP STUDY GUIDE

This group study guide is a unique companion to *What the Bible Is All About*, offering a stimulating and enjoyable opportunity for group study of the whole

Bible and its most important events and characters.

This group study guide is unique because it:

- Is based on the premise that a study of the Bible's most important events and characters is truly an exciting adventure of great value for everyone: novices and scholars, believers and seekers, male and female;
- Organizes the vast span of Bible history into four sections and the major events and characters for each section;
- Provides useful handles for looking into the meaning of historical events, identifying the greatest fact and the greatest truth for each period of Bible history;
- Includes comprehensive One-Year and Two-Year Bible Study Plans for individual study or group study after completing the course overview;
- Requires very few additional supplies for class sessions. (An overhead projector is helpful, but not necessary. Blank paper, index cards, pencils and felt-tip pens are typical of the easily secured materials, which help add variety and stimulate involvement. Suggested supplies are listed at the beginning of each session.)
- Suggests individual reading assignments to review each session, adding further reinforcement to each person's learning.

SESSION PLAN

Each of the 13 sessions is flexibly designed to be completed in one of two time schedules:

Option A—60-minute sessions.

Option B—90-minute sessions.

You will find instructions placed in boxes and marked with this clock symbol. This information provides optional learning experiences to extend this session to accommodate a 90-minute session.

OPTION ONE

This option will add 15 minutes to the session. These optional activities explore aspects of each main point that could not be addressed in the shorter time schedules.

OPTION TWO

This option will add 15 minutes to the session. These optional activities explore aspects of each main point that could not be addressed in the shorter time schedules.

A FEW TEACHING TIPS

1. Keep It Simple. Teaching people about prayer can seem like an overwhelming task. The idea of actually talking with God is truly mind-boggling and intimidating. Avoid trying to reduce prayer to a matter of following formulas or mastering a variety of techniques. Participants will remember far more if you keep the focus on one issue at a time, seeking to keep your explanations as brief and simple as possible.

2. Keep It Light. Some of the session introductory activities in this manual are fun! This is intentional. Many people who most need this course are intimidated by the Bible. Often there is fear that their own lack of knowledge will be exposed. People who are intimidated and fearful are not ready to learn. The light-hearted approaches are devices to help people relax so they can learn efficiently.

3. Keep It Significant. Because the course has some light touches does not mean its content can be handled frivolously. Keep clearly in mind—and repeatedly emphasize with your class—that this course is dealing with the awe-inspiring wonder of actually approaching the very presence of God. The insights gained in these sessions can make a big difference, not just in how people phrase their prayers, but in the overall vitality of their Christian lives.

4. Keep It Interactive. The learning activities in this manual provide a variety of involving experiences, recognizing the various learning styles which will be present in any group of adults. While some of the activities may not fit your preferred teaching style, by using this varied path to learning, you make sure that those who learn differently from the way you do will also have their needs met. A common type of involvement is having people share some of their experiences, helping one another expand understandings of various aspects of prayer and overcoming the barriers which interfere with prayer.

5. Keep It Prayerful. Both in your preparation and in each class session, pray earnestly that you and your class will be open to the truths about prayer which must be real to us if we are to enrich and deepen our communication with God.

To capture the interest of people in this course:

- Share some of your own experiences with God's Word. To succeed in leading this course, you do not need to be an expert on theology, on the Bible or on teaching methods. You do need to be honest about some of your struggles in seeking to understand and/or explain the Bible.

- Point out that while societies and cultures change, and many life experiences are different for people today than for any preceding generation, God's desire for communication with His people has remained constant in all of human history.
- Allow people to think and talk about their own experiences with God's Word. Many adults struggle with understanding and studying the Bible, finding it difficult, an obligation that causes feelings of guilt for not achieving what they feel they are expected to. This course is not a therapy workshop, but there is great value in allowing people to be open and honest in expressing their struggles. Admission of a problem is the first step in making progress toward growth.

ALTERNATE SESSION PLANS

OPTIONS FOR USING THE FOUR *WHAT THE BIBLE IS ALL ABOUT GROUP STUDY GUIDES*

Bible Overview (Eight Sessions):

What the Bible Is All About 101 Old Testament: Genesis—Esther Group Study Guide Session 2—Genesis to Joshua

What the Bible Is All About 101 Old Testament: Genesis—Esther Group Study Guide Session 8—Judges to Esther

What the Bible Is All About 102 Old Testament: Job—Malachi Group Study Guide Session 1—Job to Song of Solomon

What the Bible Is All About 102 Old Testament: Job—Malachi Group Study Guide Session 5—Isaiah to Malachi

What the Bible Is All About 201 New Testament: Matthew—Philippians Group Study Guide Session 1—The Four Gospels

What the Bible Is All About 201 New Testament: Matthew—Philippians Group Study Guide Session 6—Acts to Philippians

What the Bible Is All About 202 New Testament: Colossians—Revelation Group Study Guide Session 1—Colossians to Philemon

What the Bible Is All About 202 New Testament: Colossians—Revelation Group Study Guide Session 8—Hebrews to Revelation

Foundations of Christianity/New Christians (13 Sessions):

What the Bible Is All About 101 Old Testament: Genesis—Esther Group Study Guide Session 2—Genesis to Joshua

What the Bible Is All About 101 Old Testament: Genesis—Esther Group Study Guide Session 8—Judges to Esther

What the Bible Is All About 102 Old Testament: Job—Malachi Group Study Guide Session 1—Job to Song of Solomon

What the Bible Is All About 102 Old Testament: Job—Malachi Group Study Guide Session 5—Isaiah to Malachi

What the Bible Is All About 201 New Testament: Matthew—Philippians Group Study Guide Session 1—The Four Gospels

What the Bible Is All About 201 New Testament: Matthew—Philippians Group Study Guide Session 6—Acts to Philippians

What the Bible Is All About 202 New Testament: Colossians—Revelation Group Study Guide Session 1—Colossians to Philemon

What the Bible Is All About 202 New Testament: Colossians—Revelation Group Study Guide Session 8—Hebrews to Revelation

What the Bible Is All About 201 New Testament: Matthew—Philippians Group Study Guide Session 2—Matthew

What the Bible Is All About 201 New Testament: Matthew—Philippians Group Study Guide Session 5—John

What the Bible Is All About 201 New Testament: Matthew—Philippians Group Study Guide Session 8—Romans

What the Bible Is All About 201 New Testament: Matthew—Philippians Group Study Guide Session 12—Ephesians

What the Bible Is All About 102 Old Testament: Job—Malachi Group Study Guide Session 3—Psalms

Bible Overview with Old Testament Emphasis (13 Sessions):

What the Bible Is All About 101 Old Testament: Genesis—Esther Group Study Guide Session 2—Genesis to Joshua

What the Bible Is All About 101 Old Testament: Genesis—Esther Group Study Guide Session 8—Judges to Esther

What the Bible Is All About 102 Old Testament: Job—Malachi Group Study Guide Session 1—Job to Song of Solomon

What the Bible Is All About 102 Old Testament: Job—Malachi Group Study Guide Session 5—Isaiah to Malachi

What the Bible Is All About 201 New Testament: Matthew—Philippians Group Study Guide Session 1—The Four Gospels

What the Bible Is All About 201 New Testament: Matthew—Philippians Group Study Guide Session 6—Acts to Philippians

What the Bible Is All About 202 New Testament: Colossians—Revelation Group Study Guide Session 1—Colossians to Philemon

What the Bible Is All About 202 New Testament: Colossians—Revelation Group Study Guide Session 8—Hebrews to Revelation

What the Bible Is All About 101 Old Testament: Genesis—Esther Group Study Guide

Session 4—Exodus

What the Bible Is All About 101 Old Testament: Genesis—Esther Group Study Guide Session 10—1 Samuel

What the Bible Is All About 102 Old Testament: Job—Malachi Group Study Guide Session 3—Psalms

What the Bible Is All About 102 Old Testament: Job—Malachi Group Study Guide Session 9—Daniel

What the Bible Is All About 102 Old Testament: Job—Malachi Group Study Guide Session 11—Obadiah, Jonah and Micah

Bible Overview with New Testament Emphasis (13 Sessions):

What the Bible Is All About 101 Old Testament: Genesis—Esther Group Study Guide Session 2—Genesis to Joshua

What the Bible Is All About 101 Old Testament: Genesis—Esther Group Study Guide Session 8—Judges to Esther

What the Bible Is All About 102 Old Testament: Job—Malachi Group Study Guide Session 1—Job to Song of Solomon

What the Bible Is All About 102 Old Testament: Job—Malachi Group Study Guide Session 5—Isaiah to Malachi

What the Bible Is All About 201 New Testament: Matthew—Philippians Group Study Guide Session 1—The Four Gospels

What the Bible Is All About 201 New Testament: Matthew—Philippians Group Study Guide Session 6—Acts to Philippians

What the Bible Is All About 202 New Testament: Colossians—Revelation Group Study Guide Session 1—Colossians to Philemon

What the Bible Is All About 202 New Testament: Colossians—Revelation Group Study Guide Session 8—Hebrews to Revelation

What the Bible Is All About 201 New Testament: Matthew—Philippians Group Study Guide Session 2—Matthew

What the Bible Is All About 201 New Testament: Matthew—Philippians Group Study Guide Session 5—John

What the Bible Is All About 201 New Testament: Matthew—Philippians Group Study Guide Session 7—Acts

What the Bible Is All About 201 New Testament: Matthew—Philippians Group Study Guide Session 8—Romans

What the Bible Is All About 201 New Testament: Matthew—Philippians Group Study Guide Session 12—Ephesians

FOR 11-SESSION COURSES

What the Bible Is All About 101 Old Testament: Genesis—Esther Group Study Guide:

Combine Sessions 5 and 6; combine Sessions 10 and 11.

What the Bible Is All About 102 Old Testament: Job—Malachi Group Study Guide:

Combine Sessions 10 and 11; combine Sessions 12 and 13.

What the Bible Is All About 201 New Testament: Matthew—Philippians Group Study Guide:

Combine Sessions 9 and 10; combine Sessions 12 and 13.

What the Bible Is All About 202 New Testament: Colossians—Revelation Group Study Guide:

Combine Sessions 3 and 4; combine Sessions 5 and 6.

Understanding the Bible

The purpose of this session is:
- To provide an overview of the contents of this course;
- To discover how the Bible portrays Jesus Christ as the Savior of the world.

In this session, group members will learn:
- Key truths about God's story in the Bible;
- That the whole of Scripture reveals Jesus Christ;
- The basic principle of understanding and studying the Bible;
- How to apply basic truths in Scripture to their own lives.

KEY VERSES

"And beginning with Moses and all the Prophets, he [Jesus] explained to them what was said in all the Scriptures concerning himself." Luke 24:27

"All Scripture is God-breathed and is useful for teaching, rebuking, correcting and training in righteousness, so that the man of God may be thoroughly equipped for every good work." 2 Timothy 3:16,17

BEFORE THE SESSION

- Pray for group members by name asking the Holy Spirit to teach them the spiritual truths in this course.
- Read chapter 1 in *What the Bible Is All About*.
- Prepare copies of Session 1 handouts "Key Principles for Bible Understanding and Study" and "The Bloodline of the Messiah" for every group member.
- Check off these supplies once you have secured them:
    - ____ Copies of the handout for each group member.
    - ____ Extra Bibles, pencils and paper for all group members.
    - ____ Name tags for all the group members and pens or markers to fill them out as they enter the group.
    - ____ Packet of seeds so that every group member can have at least one seed.
- If you are having a 90-minute session, then carefully read the two option sections right now and pull together any supplies you need for them.

- Read the entire session and look up every passage. Have your Bible *Tuck-In*™ ready for yourself.
- Arrive early and be ready to warmly greet each group member as he or she arrives.
- Memorize the key verses. Share them periodically in the session and ask the group to repeat them after you.

SECTION ONE: GOD'S STORY (30 MINUTES)

Objective: To overview this study of the Bible.

Take 10-12 minutes at the beginning of this course for group members to get to know one another. Divide the group into groups of four. As the group leader, give your one-minute bio first. Let the person whose birthday is next begin and go around to the right. Let each person take 30 seconds to give a brief biography. Call time at 30-second intervals to keep the groups moving. After two minutes of these bios, put the groups of four together into groups of eight. Let each person take one minute to introduce one of the persons from his or her group of four and then that person can introduce them. Take one minute for each introduction. This will take eight minutes.

Read aloud the following, doing the suggested activities as you come to them. Distribute the handout "Key Principles for Bible Understanding and Study" so group members can take notes.

The Bible is both divine and human. The thought is divine, the revelation is divine, but the expression of the communication is human.

Our study together will focus on understanding what the Bible is all about. God uses people to tell His story. "For prophecy never had its origin in the will of man, but men spoke from God as they were carried along by the Holy Spirit" (2 Peter 1:21). Tell the group to mark statement 1 on their handouts.

The Bible is a divine, progressive revelation of God to man that has been communicated through men, moving on smoothly from its beginning to its end.

Remember that Moses had more revelation about God and His plan of salvation than did Noah or Abraham. The prophets had more revelation than David, Samson or Joshua. God progressively revealed Himself as history unfolded. Yet, all of Scripture is valuable to us in understanding how God worked His plan of salvation in Jesus Christ. We read in 2 Timothy 3:16,17, "All Scripture is God-breathed and is useful for teaching, rebuking, correcting and training in righteousness, so that the man (or woman) of God may be thoroughly equipped for every good work." Tell the group to mark statement 2 on their handouts.

While having 40 authors spanning over 1600 years, the Bible is one book, one history, one story—God's story!

We might say we will be studying "who" the Bible is all about because the Bible portrays Jesus Christ as Savior of the world. God tells the story of the gift of His Son, Jesus, to save us throughout the pages of Scripture.

God's Word is filled with life, more particularly, the living revelation of Jesus Christ. God's Word is life to us. Psalm 119:25 declares, "I am laid low in the dust; preserve my life according to your word." Tell the group to mark statement 3 on their handouts.

One way we can study the Bible is by sections—law, history, poetry, major and minor prophets, Gospels, Acts, Epistles, and Revelation. Here again we find great unity for "in the volume of the book it is written about Me," says Christ. Everything points to the King!

As we study God's Word, we grow to know more and more about Christ Himself. As did with the disciples along the Emmaus Road, He does with us. "And beginning with Moses and all the Prophets, he [Jesus] explained to them what was said in all the Scriptures concerning himself" (Luke 24:27). Tell the group to mark statement 4 on their handouts.

The Old Testament is an account of a people (the Jewish people). The New Testament is an account of a Man (the Son of Man). The Jewish people were founded and nurtured by God in order to bring the Man into the world (see Genesis 12:1-3).

God promised Abraham that out of his seed or descendants, all the nations of the earth would be blessed. Paul, writing in Galatians 3:16, says, "The promises were spoken to Abraham and to his seed. The Scripture does not say 'and to seeds,' meaning many people, but 'and to your seed,' meaning one person, who is Christ." Tell the group to mark statement 4 on their handouts.

If you have a large class, break up into groups of three or four. If you have a small class under ten persons, you may do this sharing with the whole group. Ask group members to share their answers to the following:

When I read the Bible, I see Jesus _____.

As I study the Bible in this course, I hope to discover _____.

After the sharing is completed, tell them **In the coming weeks, we shall make an overview of the various books of the Bible. As we do so, we shall explore these questions:**

What is God's story of salvation in this book (or books)?

What can we learn from God's person in this book (or books) through whom God works to accomplish His purpose?

How does this book (or these books) portray Jesus Christ?

What biblical truths and principles can we apply from our study to our daily lives?

How can we pray and encourage one another in the study of the Bible and in living the Christian life?

OPTION ONE: (FOR A 90-MINUTE SESSION)

Finding Our Way Around the Bible (15 Minutes)

Say to the group:

During this course, we will be referring to specific sections of Scripture. So that we all have the same understanding and foundation for finding our way around Scripture, let's get familiar with the four major sections of the Old Testament and the four major sections of the New Testament. I will divide everyone into groups of four and write on the chalkboard, flipchart or overhead the major sections of the Old Testament. Each group will be given four pieces of blank paper for the Old Testament. Label them: OT 1, OT 2, OT 3 and OT 4.

Write the following on a chalkboard, flipchart or overhead, and then erase as the groups start learning the sections: OT 1—Law, OT 2—History, OT 3—Poetry and OT 4—Prophecy. Have group members open their Bibles to the contents page. Explain which books of the Bible belong to each section.

Memorize the topic of the section that your paper represents. Then I will erase the chalkboard, flipchart or overhead and everyone in the group will pass around the four sheets and practice saying what each section is with the help of everyone else in the group until that person knows all four sections. Then pass the paper on to the right and let that person practice until he or she knows all four sections.

When all the groups have completed the Old Testament survey of sections, then go to the NT survey in the same way. Just have them turn over their sheets of paper and label the blank sides: NT 1, NT 2, NT 3 and NT 4.

Write the following on a chalkboard, flipchart or overhead, and then erase as the groups start learning the sections: NT 1—Gospels, NT 2—History, NT 3—Epistles and NT 4—Prophecy. Have group members open their Bibles to the contents page. Explain which books of the Bible belong to each section.

Have them go through the same process until everyone in the small group has completed learning the New Testament sections.

SECTION TWO: GOD'S PERSON (20 MINUTES)

JESUS CHRIST: THE SAVIOR OF THE WORLD

Objective: To discover how the Bible portrays Jesus Christ as Savior of the world.

Ask everyone in the group to look at the handout entitled "The Bloodline of the Messiah." Then say to the group:

From Adam and Eve's fall in the garden to the resurrection of Jesus, the drama of the Bible is God seeking to bring people back to their true humanity which they have lost by turning away from God and living their lives independent from Him. In every generation, faithful people who trusted God carried within them the promise of the coming King of kings. The bloodline of the Messiah can be traced from Genesis to the Gospels.

As we've seen, the Bible has two main divisions—The Old Testament and New Testament.

With the whole group, take about five minutes and share what the group members believe are the major differences between the Old and the New Testaments. For example, the Old seems to focus on law while the New Testament emphasizes grace. The Old talks about many men and women of faith while the New Testament emphasizes the Man in whom we place our faith—Jesus Christ.

Now using a chalkboard, flipchart or overhead write these two lists. Write down the item from the Old Testament and see if the group can guess the New Testament contrast before you write it down.

Contrasts Between the Old and New Testaments

Old Testament	New Testament
Ceremonial law	Fulfillment of Law in Christ
Gathers around Sinai	Gathers around calvary
Associated with Moses	Centers on Christ
Begins with God	Begins with Christ
God's chosen people—Israel	God's people—the Church from every people, nation, tribe and people
Messiah foretold	Messiah revealed—Jesus

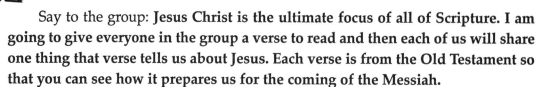

Say to the group: **Jesus Christ is the ultimate focus of all of Scripture. I am going to give everyone in the group a verse to read and then each of us will share one thing that verse tells us about Jesus. Each verse is from the Old Testament so that you can see how it prepares us for the coming of the Messiah.**

Assign each person in the group one Scripture to look up. (If there are more verses than group members, assign two verses to each person. It is not necessary that all verses be used.) Then have them report back by saying "One thing my verse revealed about Jesus Christ is that   ."

As group members share, write down on a chalkboard, flipchart or overhead the book and brief description they share about Jesus. Your list might look like the following:

Book	About Jesus
Genesis	He will rule forever

Here are the verses:

Genesis 12:1,2	Daniel 2:44
Genesis 49:10	Daniel 7:13,14
Exodus 12:21-23	Daniel 9:26
Deuteronomy 18:15	Micah 5:2
Psalm 16:10	Haggai 2:7
Psalm 42:1	Zechariah 3:8
Psalm 53	Zechariah 6:12
Psalm 110	Zechariah 9:9
Psalm 118:22	Zechariah 11:12
Isaiah 9:2,6	Zechariah 12:10
Isaiah 42:1	Malachi 3:1

OPTION TWO: (FOR A 90-MINUTE SESSION)

From Abraham's Seed (15 Minutes)

Give each person in the room a seed. You can get a packet of seeds from the grocery store or the garden center of any major store chain. Say, **Look at your seed. How many seeds do you have in your hand? Just one. How many seeds can that one seed produce?** Discuss this possibility for a moment. Now read Galatians 3:16.

Out of Adam, Noah, Abraham, Isaac, Jacob, Judah, Ruth, David and David's descendants came the Son of David—the Messiah, Jesus (see Luke 3:36,38;

Matthew 1:1-3,5,6; Romans 1:1-4). **The bloodline of the Messiah from Old to New Testaments is the story of the Seed that would become the Savior of the World.**

With the whole group discuss:

Why was the Bible written?

Ask group members to read John 20:30,31; John 1:1-4; 1 John 1:1-4; and Hebrews 1:1-4; John 8:48-59. Discuss how the Bible points completely to the Word of God, Jesus.

Is the Bible the story of humanity seeking God or the story of God seeking humanity?

Ask group members to read Deuteronomy 4:29; 2 Chronicles 7:14; Ezekiel 34:11; Matthew 6:33; Luke 19:10 and Romans 3:9-18 and 10:20. **While many passages speak of people seeking God, they all reflect God's prior efforts to reach out and His promises to reveal Himself to all who seek Him.** After this discussion, read John 3:16. **How does the seed of life in Jesus Christ get planted in us?**

Assign various group members to read Mark 4:13-20; John 3:3-8; Psalm 119:11.

Scripture says that "faith comes by hearing and hearing by the Word of God" (Romans 10:17). As we study and receive His Word, our faith grows and matures in Christ Jesus.

PURSUING GOD (5 MINUTES)

NEXT STEPS I NEED TO TAKE

Objective: To take a realistic assessment of one's relationship with Jesus and how that relationship might grow closer in the coming week.

Ask each person to look on their handout at the section entitled, "My Next Step Is...." Have each person complete the section. Share your plan. Then have group members form pairs and share how they completed this section.

PRAYER (5 MINUTES)

SEEKING GOD'S GUIDANCE IN PRAYER

Objective: To close the session in prayer for one another, asking God's power and direction in the coming week.

Praying Encouragement and Blessing

Invite the pairs to pray for one another seeking God's power to keep the commitments they have just made. If they are not comfortable praying aloud, they may pray silently. After the pairs have completed this time of prayer, invite them to pray the Aaronic blessing after you (see Numbers 6:24-26) for their partners by putting their partners' names in the blanks. Ask the partners to pray each line responsively after you have spoken it.

"The Lord bless (name) and keep (name).
The Lord make his face to shine upon (name).
and be gracious unto (name).
The Lord turn his face toward (name)
and give (name) peace. Amen."

Remind each group member after the closing prayer time when and where the group will meet next time.

Session 1 Bible *Tuck-In*™

UNDERSTANDING THE BIBLE

The purpose of this session is:

- To provide an overview of the Bible;
- To discover how Jesus Christ is revealed throughout Scripture.

KEY VERSES

"And beginning with Moses and all the Prophets, he [Jesus] explained to them what was said in all the Scriptures concerning himself." Luke 24:27

"All Scripture is God-breathed and is useful for teaching, rebuking, correcting and training in righteousness, so that the man of God may be thoroughly equipped for every good work." 2 Timothy 3:16,17

SECTION ONE: GOD'S STORY (20 MINUTES)

AN OVERVIEW OF BIBLE STUDY PRINCIPLES

- Tell the group the Bible story. Distribute the handout "Key Principles for Bible Understanding and Study" so group members can take notes. Have them fill-in their responses on the handout as you come to each principle.

— Fold —

Share your plan. Then have group members form pairs and share how they completed this section.

PRAYER (5 MINUTES)

SEEKING GOD'S GUIDANCE IN PRAYER

- Invite the pairs to pray for one another seeking God's power to keep the commitments they have just made. If they are not comfortable praying aloud, they may pray silently. After the pairs have completed this time of prayer, invite them to pray the Aaronic blessing after you (see Numbers 6:24-26) for their partners by putting their partners' names in the blanks. Ask the partners to pray each line responsively after you have spoken it.

OPTION ONE: (FOR A 90-MINUTE SESSION)

Finding Our Way Around the Bible (15 Minutes)

- Give each group four blank sheets of paper. Give instructions to the group on labeling and learning about the four sections of the Old Testament.
- When all the groups have completed the OT survey of sections, then go to the NT survey in the same way. Just have them turn over their sheets of paper and label the blank sides: NT 1, NT 2, NT 3, NT 4.
- Have them go through the same process until everyone in the small group has completely learned the NT sections.
- The following information is what you will put on a chalkboard, flipchart or overhead for each testament and then erase as the groups start learning the sections:

OT 1—Law   NT 1—Gospels
OT 2—History   NT 2—History
OT 3—Poetry   NT 3—Epistles
OT 4—Prophecy   NT 4—Prophecy

SECTION TWO: GOD'S PERSON (20 MINUTES)

JESUS CHRIST: THE SAVIOR OF THE WORLD

- Ask everyone in the group to look at the handout entitled "The Bloodline of the Messiah." Explain this to them.
- Take about five minutes and share what the group believes are the major differences between the Old and the New Testaments.
- Now go to a chalkboard, flipchart or overhead and write down the item from the Old Testament and see if the group can guess the New Testament contrast before you write it down.
- Go around the group and assign each person one Scripture to look up (if there are more verses than group members, assign two or more verses to each person) and then report back to the

---- Fold ----

group saying "One thing my verse revealed about Jesus Christ is that _____."

- As group members share, write down on a chalkboard, flipchart or overhead the book and brief description they shared about Jesus.

OPTION TWO: (FOR A 90-MINUTE SESSION)

From Abraham's Seed (15 Minutes)

- Give each person in the room a seed. You can get a packet of seeds from the grocery store or the garden center of any major store chain. Explain what the seed means.
- Discuss:

Why was the Bible written?
Ask group members to read John 20:30,31; John 1:1-4; 1 John 1:1-4; and Hebrews 1:1-4; John 8:48-59. Discuss how the Bible points completely to the Word of God, Jesus.

Is the Bible the story of humanity seeking God or the story of God seeking humanity?
Ask group members to read Deuteronomy 4:29; 2 Chronicles 7:14; Ezekiel 34:11; Matthew 6:33; Luke 19:10 and Romans 3:9-18 and 10:20. **While many passages speak of people seeking God, they all reflect God's prior efforts to reach out and His promises to reveal Himself to all who seek. After this discussion, read John 3:16.**

How does the seed of life in Jesus Christ get planted in us?
Assign various group members to read Mark 4:13-20; John 3:3-8; Psalm 119:11.
Scripture says that faith comes by hearing and hearing by the Word of God (see Romans 10:17). As we study and receive His Word, our faith grows and matures in Christ Jesus.

PURSUING GOD (5 MINUTES)

NEXT STEPS I NEED TO TAKE

- Ask each person to look on their handout at the section entitled, "My Next Step Is...." Have each person complete the section.

KEY PRINCIPLES FOR BIBLE UNDERSTANDING AND STUDY

Put an X on each line closest to your response to each statement.

✓1. The Bible is both divine and human. The thought is divine, the revelation is divine, but the expression of the communication is human. (Note 2 Peter 1:21.)

_____

I know that!   I vaguely remember that!   I didn't know that!

2. The Bible is a divine, progressive revelation of God to man that has been communicated through men, moving on smoothly from its beginning to its end.

_____

I know that!   I vaguely remember that!   I didn't know that!

3. While having 40 authors spanning over 1600 years, the Bible is one book, one history, one story—God's story!

_____

I know that!   I vaguely remember that!   I didn't know that!

4. One way we can study the Bible is by sections—law, history, poetry, major and minor prophets, Gospels, Acts, Epistles, and Revelation. Here again we find great unity for "in the volume of the book it is written of Me," says Christ. Everything points to the King!

_____

I know that!   I vaguely remember that!   I didn't know that!

5. The Old Testament is an account of a people (the Jewish people). The New Testament is an account of a Man (the Son of Man). The Jewish people were founded and nurtured by God in order to bring the Man into the world (see Genesis 12:1-3).

_____

I know that!   I vaguely remember that!   I didn't know that!

CONTINUED

MY NEXT STEP IS...

In the coming weeks, I commit myself to: (check as many as you are willing to commit to.)

❑ Read the Bible readings assigned for each day during each week.

❑ Memorize a key verse from each book of the Bible.

❑ Learn the books of the Bible in order.

❑ Pray daily for instruction and guidance from God's Holy Spirit in my Bible study and application.

❑ Pray for this group and our group leader.

Before next week's session, read:

Monday: God's Word (John 1; 1 John 1)

Tuesday: The Power of the Word (Romans 10; 1 Timothy 3:15; Hebrews 4:12)

Wednesday: The Guidance of His Word (Psalm 119)

Thursday: The Perfect Word of God (Psalm 19:7-14)

Friday: The Seed of the Word (Mark 4)

Saturday: The Eternal Word (Revelation 1)

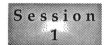
THE BLOODLINE OF THE MESSIAH

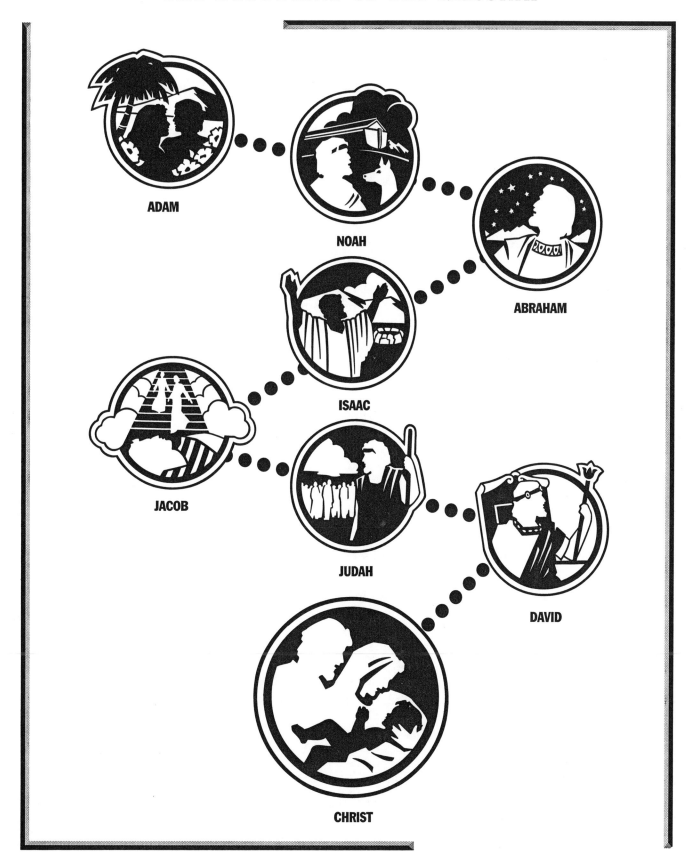

Understanding God's Story in the Old Testament

The purpose of this session is:
- To provide an overview of the Old Testament;
- To discover how the Bible portrays Jesus Christ in the Old Testament.

In this session, group members will learn:
- Key truths about God's story in the Old Testament;
- That the whole of Scripture portrays Jesus Christ as the coming Messiah;
- The basic principle of revelation;
- How to apply basic truths in Scripture to their own lives.

KEY VERSES

"Your word, O LORD, is eternal; it stands firm in the heavens. Your faithfulness continues through all generations; you established the earth, and it endures. Your word is a lamp to my feet and a light for my path." Psalm 119:89,90,105

"In the past God spoke to our forefathers through the prophets at many times and in various ways, but in these last days he has spoken to us by his Son, whom he appointed heir of all things, and through whom he made the universe." Hebrews 1:1,2

"The LORD has made his salvation known and revealed his righteousness to the nations. He has remembered his love and his faithfulness to the house of Israel; all the ends of the earth have seen the salvation of our God." Psalm 98:2,3

BEFORE THE SESSION

- Pray for group members by name asking the Holy Spirit to teach them the spiritual truths in this session.
- Read chapter 13 and skim chapters 2-12 in *What the Bible Is All About*.
- Prepare copies of Session 2 handouts, "An Overview of Old Testament History"

and "The Bible—A Library of Smaller Books" for every group member.

- Prepare copies of Session 1 handout, "The Bloodline of the Messiah" for every group member.
- Check off these supplies once you have secured them:

____ Make copies for pairs in your group of Session 2 handout, entitled, "The Bible—A Library of Smaller Books." Cut these handouts along the dotted lines. Shuffle the six sections of each handout thoroughly and paper clip them together. The pairs will try to put these in the correct order. Keep one complete, uncut copy for yourself.

____ Have extra Bibles, pencil and paper for the group members.

- If you are having a 90-minute session, then carefully read the two option sections right now and pull together any supplies you need for them.
- Read the entire session and look up every passage. Have your Bible *Tuck-In*™ ready for yourself.
- Arrive early and be ready to warmly greet each group member as he or she arrives.
- Memorize the key verses. Share them periodically in the session and ask the group to repeat them after you.

SECTION ONE: GOD'S STORY (25 MINUTES)

OLD TESTAMENT: GOD'S STORY

Objective: To discover how God's story progresses and unfolds from Creation to Christ.

Read aloud the following, doing the suggested activities as you come to them. Distribute the handout "Overview of Old Testament History" so group members can take notes.

The Bible is a book of 66 books written by at least 40 authors over a period of 1,600 years.

Over the next few months, we shall explore together how all these books present one central theme—Jesus Christ is the Savior of the world. Let's review the order of these books just to get you somewhat comfortable in finding your way around the Bible.

Have group members form groups of 6-8. Give each group one set of Session 2 handout that have been cut along the dotted lines and shuffled together. Give them two minutes to try to put these books in the right order. Then give the right order to the whole group.

The Bible tells the story of Jesus Christ. From humanity's separation from God in the Garden of Eden until the end of history in Revelation, the Bible tells God's story of seeking a relationship with us.

You may have wondered how all the Bible fits together. You will learn how God's Story was revealed and enacted through people, events and nations over thousands of years. Let's look over the order of these historical periods.

Peak One begins God's story in the Old Testament with the Creation and progresses through the Fall, Flood and call of Abraham (Genesis 1—12).

From creation, to the establishing of nations, to the start of God's people through Abraham, God lays the foundation for seeking and saving humanity and all of creation.

Ask group members to form groups of four. Have each person in his or her small group pick a number from one to four. During the rest of the session, refer to the persons in the groups that need to do a particular thing by their numbers. Make certain that everyone has a Bible. Give these instructions:

Ones represent Creation and the Fall; twos are Babel; threes are the Flood and fours are the Call of Abram—Abraham (if some groups have a fifth person, have the fives work with the fours). **Look in the first 12 chapters of the book of Genesis. Find the chapter where your subject starts. Skim over the basic facts about that story. Share a one-sentence summary with your group in order—one to four—of the beginning of your story. You have four minutes to complete this.** After four minutes, ask all the ones **Where do we find the Creation and the Fall?** Repeat for the other three sections.

Peak Two covers the call of Abraham to His people coming out of Egypt (Genesis 12—50).

Scholars usually call this the Patriarchal Period. God called the patriarchs—the fathers of His people, Israel—to enter into a covenant with Him, to have a relationship of faith and trust in Him. As they trusted Him in obedience, He revealed His promises and purposes to the patriarchs.

Ones, skim over the section headings starting in Genesis 12 on the life of Abraham and jot some of them down for your group; twos discover the patriarch whose story begins in Genesis 21 and skim over the major headings in his life; threes start in Genesis 27 finding the name of your patriarch and some of the main subjects in his life; fours look at the rest of Genesis from chapter 37 discovering the main character and what happened to him and the people of God.

Take about four minutes to skim over your sections and then take one minute each to share your discoveries with the other group members.

As the groups do these discoveries, go from group to group just to answer any questions they may have and help in any way needed. After four minutes, tell the group that they should be sharing their information with one another by now.

Invite volunteers to share two or three facts about the character in their designated chapter.

Peak Three covers the coming out of Egypt to the coronation of Saul. God worked through His leaders to bring Israel out of bondage in Egypt into the Promised Land (Exodus—1 Samuel 11).

There are several key people in God's Story. Moses lead Israel out of Egypt and to Mount Sinai where God gave His Law and established worship. God used Joshua to lead Israel out of the wilderness, across the Jordan and into possession of the Promised Land. God used judges to bring Israel back to Him and battle Israel's enemies. Finally, God used the judge Samuel to anoint Saul the first king for Israel.

Instruct ones to skim over Exodus 1—20 and Numbers 9—14 to see some highlights from the Exodus through the wanderings of Israel in the wilderness. Twos are to skim over Joshua. Threes are to skim over Judges. Fours are to skim over Ruth and the first 11 chapters of 1 Samuel. Tell them to look for major headings and not for details. They have four minutes to skim over their sections and one minute each to report back to the group.

Peak Four spans God's Story from Saul's coronation to captivity in Babylon (1 Samuel 12—31; 2 Samuel; 1 and 2 Kings; 1 and 2 Chronicles and the prophets).

Saul started his walk with God great but finished in rebellion and destruction. Isn't that how it often is in life? It's not how you start, but how you finish that counts. On the other hand, David sinned greatly through his life but always repented and returned to God. He finished God's purpose for his life. David's son, Solomon, started great but finished worshiping idols. The Kingdom divided. The Northern Kingdom had one wicked king after another, worshiped pagan idols and was utterly lost and carried into captivity by Assyria in 722 B.C. The Southern Kingdom of Judah, at times, had righteous kings like Hezekiah, Uzziah and Josiah. However, Judah also fell away from God and was carried into captivity by Babylon in 586 B.C.

In Peak Five, God preserved a remnant of His people in captivity to return and rebuild Jerusalem and the Temple with Nehemiah and Ezra's leadership, thus reestablishing worship of the living God (Ezra and Nehemiah).

God's Story in the Old Testament is one in which He seeks out a people who will trust, love and obey Him living in righteousness and holiness. His Story is one of peaks and valleys. The mountain peaks are God working in history to redeem and reestablish a relationship or covenant with His people. The valleys are humanity's and Israel's times of breaking the relationship and rejecting God.

Think of it this way. I will put on the chalkboard, flipchart or overhead a **peak and you guess the valley**. The peaks are listed in plain type. You write them down. The valleys are in *italics*. Let the group try to guess what the valley is before you write it down. Invite them to take notes on their handouts.

Peaks: God Seeks His People	Valleys: People Reject God
Creation and Eden	*The fall of Adam and Eve*
Abel is righteous	*Cain murders Abel*
Noah is righteous	*Wicked humanity and the Flood*
Abraham, Isaac and Jacob covenant with God	*Israel in slavery in Egypt*
The Exodus and Mount Sinai with the Law	*The golden calf*
Conquering the Promised Land	*Worshiping idols; wilderness wanderings*
Establishing the Kingdom under Saul, David and Solomon; building the Temple	*The divided Kingdom and exile*
Returning to Jerusalem, rebuilding the walls and the Temple	*Greek and Roman rule of Israel*

OPTION ONE: (FOR A 90-MINUTE SESSION)

YOUR FAVORITE STORY FROM HISTORY (15 MINUTES)

Say to the group:

History is God's Story, or His Story. His Story in the Old Testament is filled with many wonderful and powerful stories about how God acted and spoke. His Story is also your story. How has God worked and spoken in your personal story? What I would like you to share briefly is how God has worked and spoken in your life to bring you into a relationship with Him. Also share your favorite story from the Old Testament and why it is your favorite. So starting with the fours and counting down, take about three minutes each to share about how God has worked in your story to bring you into a relationship with Him—you may simply be seeking Him now, or you may be a new believer, or you may have trusted Jesus for years. Whatever the case, just share simply where you are right now in your story with the Lord. Be honest because our only expectation here is that wherever each person is right now in his or her relationship with Jesus Christ is that you are seeking to grow closer to Him by being here.

So, you are sharing two things:

What is your favorite Old Testament story and why?

Where you are in your relationship with Jesus Christ right now—seeking, new, growing.

After about six minutes, remind the group that at least two people should have shared. After 12 minutes, close the sharing and invite the whole group to pray this prayer with you.

Lord Jesus, I seek to know You and grow closer to You through Your Word. Through Your Holy Spirit, teach me Your truth and reveal Yourself to me in Your Word. I ask this in the powerful name of Jesus, Amen.

SECTION TWO: GOD'S SON (25 MINUTES)

JESUS CHRIST: THE MESSIAH REVEALED IN THE OLD TESTAMENT

Objective: To provide an overview of the bloodline (ancestry) of the Messiah through God's Story in the Old Testament

Give everyone a copy of the handout, "The Bloodline of the Messiah."

Say, **This really is the wonder of the Bible—that it has but one theme, and that theme is the Lord Jesus Christ. Each of the Gospels, which tell the story of His life, take us back into the Old Testament to help us fully understand His mission.**

Mark **starts his story of Jesus' life by taking us back to the prophet Isaiah: "The beginning of the gospel about Jesus Christ, the Son of God. It is written in Isaiah the prophet: 'I will send my messenger ahead of you, who will prepare your way'" (Mark 1:1,2).**

Matthew **begins by stating: "A record of the genealogy of Jesus Christ the son of David, the son of Abraham" (Matthew 1:1).**

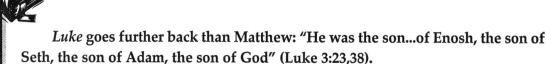

Luke goes further back than Matthew: "He was the son...of Enosh, the son of Seth, the son of Adam, the son of God" (Luke 3:23,38).

John begins, "In the beginning was the Word, and the Word was with God, and the Word was God" (John 1:1).

After His death and resurrection, Jesus explained those events to two disciples by "beginning with Moses and all the Prophets, he explained to them what was said in all the Scriptures concerning himself" (Luke 24:27).

If we open a novel in the middle of the book and begin to read about the hero, we soon find we have to go back to the beginning if we are to understand the story. As you study the New Testament, you quickly find that God's plan of redemption was no afterthought, but it was a clear unfolding of His eternal purpose.

The Old Testament is filled with examples of God working out that purpose in preparation for sending His own Son in human flesh. God's plan was not to redeem humanity by giving us rules or by establishing a philosophy of life, but by living among us in order to become the perfect sacrifice for our sinful rebellion against God. Thus, one of the most illuminating of all biblical studies is to trace the lineage of the Messiah, discovering along the way, not just a family tree, but an amazing series of incidents that gradually reveal the fullness of God's purpose.

Divide the class into seven groups. Assign each group to read about one segment of "The Bloodline of Messiah":

1. The Human Race of Adam (Genesis 3:15; Luke 3:38; 1 Corinthians 15:45; Hebrews 2:17,18)
2. Preacher of Righteousness, Noah (Genesis 6:5-10; 9:8-13; Luke 3:36; Hebrews 11:7)
3. Father of a Nation, Abraham (Genesis 15:5,6; 18:18,19; Luke 1:72,73)
4. Promised Heir, Isaac (Genesis 21:12; 22:15-18; Galatians 4:28)
5. Branch of Jacob (Genesis 28:1-4; Numbers 24:17-19; Luke 1:33)
6. Tribe of Judah (Genesis 38:13-18,27-29; 49:10; Matthew 1:3; Revelation 5:5)
7. Family of David (2 Samuel 7:16; Psalm 89:35-37; Ezekiel 37:24,25; Matthew 1:1; 12:22,23)

Instruct the groups to look in their assigned verses for clues about the purpose of God as shown by that link in Messiah's lineage.

Allow five to seven minutes for groups to read and talk, then invite a volunteer from each group to report on their findings. Taken as a group, the ancestors of Messiah reflect the full range of human sin and response to God's loving forgiveness.

Summarize this overview of the Old Testament narrative. **The New Testament shows Jesus Christ as the consummation of the bloodline. Jesus is the "son of man," partaking of our nature, dying for our sins, tasting and conquering death on our behalf. As the Son of David, legal son of the royal line, He is coming back**

to reign, holding dominion "from sea to sea and from the River to the ends of the earth" (Psalm 72:8).

Notice in Matthew 1:1 Jesus is spoken of as the Son of David and the Son of Abraham. He is not called the Son of any of those who follow those men. Remember, both Abraham and David were specifically promised a son. The immediate fulfillment of that promise to each man was disappointing. Neither Isaac nor Solomon fulfilled the promise of God, but Jesus more than fulfilled it. Both Isaac and Solomon were imperfect. Jesus is perfect. In Him, God's promise is fulfilled.

OPTION TWO: (FOR A 90-MINUTE SESSION)

Your Spiritual Peaks and Valleys (15 Minutes)

Return to the quartets formed earlier in this session. Say, **Every personal spiritual journey has peaks and valleys just as Israel's journey with God in the Old Testament. Reflect on your spiritual journey. On the back of your handout, chart the peaks and valleys of your spiritual journey. Some of the peaks may be times you have been really close to God or had a mountaintop experience with Him. The valleys may have been crises or desert experiences in your walk with God when He seemed far away from you. Label some of those ups and downs. You have about five minutes to do this.**

After five minutes, instruct the groups: **Beginning with the ones and going in order, to share at least one valley and one peak experience.** If time permits, they may share more.

PURSUING GOD (5 MINUTES)

NEXT STEPS I NEED TO TAKE

Objective: To take a realistic assessment of one's relationship with Jesus and how that relationship might grow closer in the coming week.

In the small groups, have each person share his or her completion to the following sentence:

One way I would like to grow closer to Christ through this study in the coming weeks is _____.

PRAYER (5 MINUTES)

SEEKING GOD'S GUIDANCE IN PRAYER

Objective: To close this session with praise and prayer.

Have the whole group form a circle. Go around the circle beginning with you, the leader, and moving clockwise to share one praise to God as a result of something learned in this session. Assure people that if someone else mentions the same thing they planned to share that they should go ahead and repeat it.

I praise God for learning that _____.

After everyone has shared, close the group in prayer asking the Lord to fill them with wisdom and knowledge as they learn His Story in the coming weeks.

Session 2 Bible *Tuck-In*™

UNDERSTANDING GOD'S STORY IN THE OLD TESTAMENT

The purpose of this session is:

- To provide an overview of God's story in the Old Testament;
- To discover how Jesus Christ is revealed in the Old Testament.

KEY VERSES

"Your word, O LORD, is eternal; it stands firm in the heavens. Your faithfulness continues through all generations; you established the earth, and it endures. Your word is a lamp to my feet and a light for my path." Psalm 119:89,90,105

"In the past God spoke to our forefathers through the prophets at many times and in various ways, but in these last days he has spoken to us by his Son, whom he appointed heir of all things, and through whom he made the universe." Hebrews 1:1,2

"The LORD has made his salvation known and revealed his righteousness to the nations. He has remembered his love and his faithfulness to the house of Israel; all the ends of the earth have seen the salvation of our God." Psalm 98:2,3

PRAYER (5 MINUTES)

SEEKING GOD'S GUIDANCE IN PRAYER

- Have the whole group form a circle. Go around the circle beginning with you, the leader, and moving clockwise to share one praise to God as a result of something learned in this session. Assure people that if someone else mentions the same thing they planned to share that they should go ahead and repeat it. **I praise God for learning that** _____

- After everyone has shared, close the group in a prayer asking the Lord to fill them with wisdom and knowledge as they learn His story in the coming weeks.

SECTION ONE: GOD'S STORY (25 MINUTES)

OLD TESTAMENT: GOD'S STORY

- Tell the group the Bible story doing the suggested activities as you come to them. Distribute the handout "An Overview of God's Story in the Old Testament" so group members can take notes.

OPTION ONE: (FOR A 90-MINUTE SESSION)

Your Favorite Story from History (15 Minutes)

- Give the group instructions on how to tell:

  What is your favorite Old Testament story and why?
  Where you are in your relationship with Jesus Christ right now—seeking, new, growing?

  After about six minutes remind the group that at least two people should have shared. After 12 minutes close the sharing and invite the whole group to pray this prayer with you.

  Lord Jesus, I seek to know You and grow closer to You through Your Word. Through Your Holy Spirit, teach me Your truth and reveal Yourself to me in Your Word. I ask this in the powerful name of Jesus. Amen.

SECTION TWO: GOD'S PERSON (25 MINUTES)

JESUS CHRIST: THE MESSIAH REVEALED IN THE OLD TESTAMENT

- Give everyone in the group a copy of the handout, "The Bloodline of the Messiah."
- Share the background material for this exercise.
- Divide the class into seven groups for each section of the Bloodline of the Messiah and assign the Bible readings.
- Have the groups report back after about seven minutes.

OPTION TWO: (FOR A 90-MINUTE SESSION)

Your Spiritual Peaks and Valleys (15 Minutes)

- Return to the groups of four formed earlier in this session.
- Give instructions on how to chart the peaks and valleys of their spiritual lives.
- After five minutes, instruct the groups: **Beginning with the ones and going around the group in order, share at least one valley and one peak experience.** If time permits, they may share more.

PURSUING GOD (5 MINUTES)

NEXT STEPS I NEED TO TAKE

- In the small groups, have each person share the completion to the following sentence:

  One way I would like to grow closer to Christ through this study in the coming weeks is

  _____

An Overview of God's Story in the Old Testament

1. The Bible is a book of 66 books written by at least 40 authors over a period of 1600 years!

   Notes:

2. The Bible tells the story of Jesus Christ. From humanity's separation from God in the Garden of Eden until the end of history in Revelation, the Bible tells God's Story of seeking a relationship with us!

   Notes:

3. Peak One begins God's story in the Old Testament with the Creation and progresses through the Fall, Flood and call of Abraham (Genesis 1—12).

   Notes:

4. Peak Two covers the call of Abraham to coming out of Egypt (Genesis 12—50).

   Notes:

CONTINUED

5. Peak Three covers the coming out of Egypt to the coronation of Saul. God worked through His leaders to bring Israel out of bondage in Egypt into the Promised Land (Exodus—1 Samuel 11).

Notes:

6. Peak Four spans God's Story from Saul's coronation to captivity in Babylon (1 Samuel 12—31; 2 Samuel; 1 and 2 Kings; 1 and 2 Chronicles and the prophets).

Notes:

7. In Peak Five, God preserved a remnant of His people in captivity to return and rebuild Jerusalem and the Temple with Nehemiah and Ezra's leadership, thus reestablishing worship of the living God (Ezra and Nehemiah).

Notes:

Before next week's session, read:
Sunday: Creation (Genesis 1:1-5;26-31; 2:7-22)
Monday: Fall (Genesis 3:1-24)
Tuesday: Deluge (Genesis 6:1-7; 7:7-24; 8:6-11; 9:1-16)
Wednesday: Beginning of Languages (Genesis 11:1-9)
Thursday: The Abrahamic Call and Covenant (Genesis 12:1-9; 13:14-18; 15:1-21; 17:4-8; 22:15-20; 26:1-5; 28:10-15)
Friday: Story of Joseph (Genesis 37:1-36; 42)
Saturday: Jacob's Final Blessing (Genesis 49)

THE BIBLE—A LIBRARY OF SMALLER BOOKS

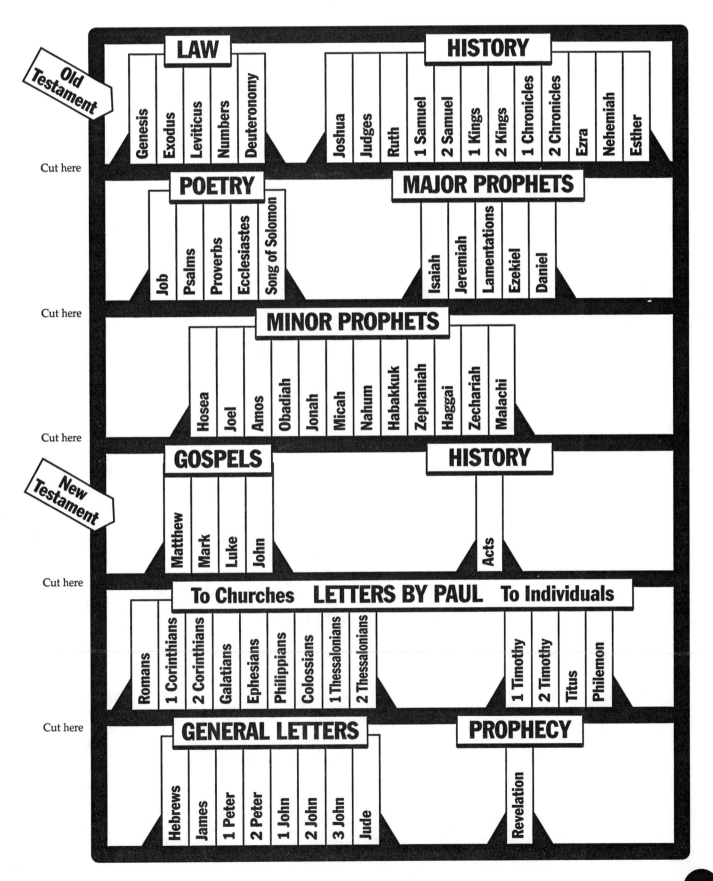

Old Testament

LAW
Genesis · Exodus · Leviticus · Numbers · Deuteronomy

HISTORY
Joshua · Judges · Ruth · 1 Samuel · 2 Samuel · 1 Kings · 2 Kings · 1 Chronicles · 2 Chronicles · Ezra · Nehemiah · Esther

Cut here

POETRY
Job · Psalms · Proverbs · Ecclesiastes · Song of Solomon

MAJOR PROPHETS
Isaiah · Jeremiah · Lamentations · Ezekiel · Daniel

Cut here

MINOR PROPHETS
Hosea · Joel · Amos · Obadiah · Jonah · Micah · Nahum · Habakkuk · Zephaniah · Haggai · Zechariah · Malachi

Cut here

New Testament

GOSPELS
Matthew · Mark · Luke · John

HISTORY
Acts

Cut here

To Churches   LETTERS BY PAUL   To Individuals
Romans · 1 Corinthians · 2 Corinthians · Galatians · Ephesians · Philippians · Colossians · 1 Thessalonians · 2 Thessalonians · 1 Timothy · 2 Timothy · Titus · Philemon

Cut here

GENERAL LETTERS
Hebrews · James · 1 Peter · 2 Peter · 1 John · 2 John · 3 John · Jude

PROPHECY
Revelation

Understanding Genesis

The purpose of this session is:
- To provide an overview of the book of Genesis;
- To discover how Jesus Christ is revealed in Genesis as our Creator-God.

In this session, group members will learn:
- Key truths about God's story in the book of Genesis;
- That Jesus Christ is revealed in Genesis;
- The basic principle of faith—trusting in God—as revealed in Abraham's relationship with God;
- How to apply basic truths in Genesis to their own lives.

KEY VERSES

"In the beginning God created the heavens and the earth." Genesis 1:1

"I will make you into a great nation and I will bless you; I will make your name great, and you will be a blessing. I will bless those who bless you, and whoever curses you I will curse; and all the peoples on earth will be blessed through you." Genesis 12:2,3

"In the beginning was the Word, and the Word was with God and the Word was God. He was with God in the beginning. Through him all things were made; without him nothing was made that has been made." John 1:1-3

BEFORE THE SESSION

- Pray for group members by name asking the Holy Spirit to teach them the spiritual truths in Genesis.
- Read chapter 2 in *What the Bible Is All About.*
- Prepare copies of Session 3 handouts "An Overview of Genesis" and "Whom Do You Trust?" for every group member.
- Check off these supplies once you have secured them:
  - ____ cotton balls
  - ____ paper basket
  - ____ yardstick, ruler or measuring tape
  - ____ Polaroid camera and film enough to take a picture of everyone in the group

- If you are having a 90-minute session, carefully read the two option sections right now and pull together any supplies you need for them.
- Read the entire session and look up every passage. Have your Bible *Tuck-In*™ ready for yourself.
- Arrive early and be ready to warmly greet each group member as he or she arrives.
- Even though this is the third session, continue to have name tags for all group members.
- Memorize the key verses. Share them periodically in the session and ask the group to repeat them after you.

Section One: God's Story (25 Minutes)

Genesis: Beginnings

Objective: To tell God's story in Genesis so that the group members will understand that God desired a covenant relationship with people and repeatedly sought to restore that covenant relationship.

As people arrive, take Polaroid pictures of your class members. Keep all the photos and then pass out half of the photos to the group. Tell the ones receiving a photo to be certain that it is not theirs or their spouse's. Have each person with a photo find the person whose picture he or she has. Share your own one-minute personal history of your life covering the past ten years. Have both partners share their own one-minute personal histories. Let the person in the photo go first.

Read aloud the following, doing the suggested activities as you come to them. Distribute Session 3 handout, "An Overview of Genesis" so group members can take notes.

The Bible Tells God's Story.

God acts. God speaks. People respond. Other religions tell of people seeking a god, but the Bible reveals how the one true God seeks out a relationship with people from the beginning of history to its climax. Throughout history God's mighty acts and words reveal Himself and His plan of salvation. We do not discover God who is off in the distance. Rather God reveals Himself to us (see Romans 3:9-18; 10:20). The Bible records God's Story for us.

God created (see Genesis 1).

Sound simple? Well, that one ultimate truth sets the Bible apart from every other ancient religion. Other cultures started with material and many gods who came out of that material. But the Bible tells the story of one God—the God of Abraham, Isaac and Jacob, the everlasting God who had no beginning and has no end, the Creator-God who created out of nothing everything that exists.

God created people in His image (see Genesis 1:26-28).

This does not mean we are God, but that we are created in God's likeness. We are able to create, love, feel, think, aspire to meaning, beauty and truth, and relate to God spiritually. However, we don't like the picture. We try to change our image from God's likeness to our own. Take a photo and tear it up. Throw the pieces out over the group. Ask group members to pick up the scattered pieces and give them back to you. **After the Fall when Adam and Eve rebelled against God, broke the covenant and rejected the relationship, only the pieces of a broken image remained. Oh yes, hope also remained. We'll explore that hope later. After the Fall, only God could put the pieces back together again and He proceeded to do just that! We will discover how, in Jesus, God gave us the perfect picture of Himself.**

From the beginning, God desired and willed a relationship with people (see Genesis 2:1-25; 3:8).

"Covenant" is a Bible word describing God's relationship with us. Say "covenant" (response). So what is a covenant? A covenant is an unchangeable agreement between God and His people that states the responsibilities and obligations of their relationship.

Have group members form groups of three or four. Give a blank piece of paper to each group. Instruct the groups: **If you could write a contract or agreement between you and God describing what He would do for you and what you would do for Him, what would be in that contract or agreement? Get suggestions from one another in your group on what might be included. Draw a line down the middle of your paper. Put "God" at the top of the left column and "People" at the top of the right column. You are humanity's legal representative. Now make a list down both columns describing God's and people's obligations in the contract. Take about three minutes to do this.**

Now ask the group for a volunteer who is willing to share what he or she wrote. After the volunteer has read his or her agreement, invite the class to share briefly other items or obligations they put in their contracts. Discuss and reach a group consensus on the main demand of God on Adam and Eve and their responsibility in light of that demand (see Genesis 2:16,17). Write that on the volunteer's paper. Explain to the group: **We are now going to see how God writes contracts which the Bible calls "covenants."**

God created; people rebelled—the Fall (see Genesis 3).

God created the universe and put people in a perfect relationship with Him. The agreement or covenant was simple to choose between life and death—between the truth of God and lies of Satan. Two trees. Two choices. One life. The other, death. One God. The other, people would be their own god. History pivoted on human choice. Adam and Eve, people, all of us chose death. Like Adam and Eve, all of us have rebelled against God and brought suffering and spiritual death upon ourselves. God's Story revealed in the Bible tells how a loving God spoke and acted in history to redeem and to restore the relationship between Himself and people.

Show a picture of yourself. Ask a group member, **Is this me?** When they say "Yes," say, **Of course it is not me. I am me. This is only a representation or image of me.** Have fun with this and then explain the following:

God judges wickedness—the Flood (see Genesis 6—9).

In the aftermath of the Fall, everywhere God looked, people were drowning in evil. God grieved that He had ever created people. Yet in the midst of an ocean of sin, one man remained righteous—Noah. Washing away an ocean of human wickedness with a flood was God's judgment on people. But one man, one family, one boatload of life was saved. God loved us enough to spare people through just one man. It would not be the last time that God would save people with just one man (see Romans 5:12-21). Millennia later God would love us so much that one Man—Jesus—would save everyone who calls upon His name from their sin and rebellion against God and the ark within which He would keep us safe would be called "the Church."

On a chalkboard, flipchart or overhead, write the word "Covenant" and then list the way a relationship between people and God progressed. Ask the group to guess what the sign and promise of each covenant would be before you write it down.

Covenant Relationship	Sign	Promise
Creation/Edenic	Tree of Life	Life
Fall/Adamic	Curse of Toil and Childbirth	Conquer Satan
Noah	Rainbow	Never again to flood the earth

Ask, **Who has the strongest arm?** Have a wastepaper basket at the front of the room and give two group members some cotton balls. Ask them to stand at the back of the room and throw the cotton balls into the basket. Of course, it will be impossible. Then walk with the basket to the group members. Stand right in front of them. Help them throw the cotton ball right into the basket. Have fun with this. Laugh at how easy it is to make a basket when the gap is closed and help is given.

God seeks people, but people cannot reach God by human effort (see Genesis 10).

That's the story of the tower of Babel. The Fall is the story of how Adam and Eve rebelled and failed to "be like God." The story of Babel tells how people failed in their attempt to reach God. The chasm of sin from humans to God can never be bridged by our efforts. God will ultimately bridge the gap—not with a tower of human effort but with the Cross of divine love.

God called; Abraham trusted (see Genesis 11—12).

God chose one person, Abraham, to begin a project of building a people that would bring God's salvation to all peoples. God called Abraham to leave his home in Ur of the Chaldees and go to a new land. God promised He would make Abraham a great people and a great land, and he would use him to bless all peoples. In faith, Abraham trusted God, left his old gods, culture and lifestyle behind and followed God.

Through Abraham, Isaac and Jacob, God made a covenant with a family to be His people in order to "bless" all peoples (see Genesis 12; 15; 17; 22; 26; 28).

God promised to bless Abraham and to bless the peoples of the earth through Abraham. "To bless" means to bring salvation and prosperity—all the benefits and heritage of a relationship with God. The covenant relationship with people was being rebuilt, rooted in God's promise and human faith. History again pivots on one man. The Apostle Paul would later write that through one man—Adam—all sinned. Now the hope of people pivots on one man—Abraham. In his old age, God asked Abraham to sacrifice Isaac, the son God had promised. Would Abraham trust God enough to obey? Adam had failed his test. Noah had obeyed God when commanded to build an ark. Now it was Abraham's turn. Abraham's test was to believe God's promise even when He told Abraham to sacrifice his son Isaac. What would you have done?

Stop the narrative at this point. As a class, briefly discuss:
Why did Isaac go along with his father? How would you describe Isaac's faith? Why did God choose such a difficult test for Abraham and Isaac?
Add to your covenant chart on the chalkboard, flipchart or overhead:

Abraham	Faith and Circumcision	Your offspring will bless (bring salvation to) the nations

From a family to a nation, God protected His people called Israel in the land of Egypt (see Genesis 37—50).

Through an amazing set of circumstances, Jacob's son Joseph becomes a ruler in

Egypt. Jacob and all of his sons go to Egypt to escape famine and be secure. As we leave God's Story in Genesis, God has begun to restore His covenant relationship with people through Abraham's family, a family that will grow into a nation called Israel. Israel's security will become bondage and the next test of faith is just around the corner.

OPTION ONE: (FOR A 90-MINUTE SESSION)

The Patriarchal Period (15 Minutes)

Say to the group, **The patriarchal period of Israel covers the time from Abraham through Joseph. The patriarchs were the "covenant fathers" of the Hebrew people. The four patriarchs in Genesis are Abraham, Isaac, Jacob and Joseph. God makes a covenant with Abraham and restates it to Isaac and Jacob. A covenant is a legal agreement between two persons or parties that establishes a binding relationship between them. This covenant established the descendants of Abraham as the people of God—Israel, or the Hebrews. Let's examine this covenant of promise.**

Divide the whole group into four small groups. Assign each small group one of the following passages: Genesis 12:1-3; 17:1-8; 26:1-5; 28:13-15. Make certain that every small group has pencil, paper and one person chosen to be the recorder. Ask each group to take two minutes to list all of the promises made to Abraham or his descendants by God in the passage they have been assigned.

After two minutes for group members to read and summarize, invite someone to share a promise from the covenants. List the promises on a chalkboard, flipchart or overhead under the heading "God's Promises to Abraham." That list, when complete, would include a summary of this list from Genesis 12:1-3; 17:1-8; 26:1-5; 28:13-15.

God's Promises to the Patriarchs

I will make your (Abraham's) name great.
You will be a blessing.
I will bless those that bless you.
I will curse those that curse you.
All peoples on the earth will be blessed through you.
I will greatly increase your numbers.
You (Abraham) will be the father of many peoples.
I will make you fruitful.

I will make peoples of you and kings will come from you.

I will establish my covenant as an everlasting covenant.

I will give you the whole land of Canaan as an everlasting possession.

I will be your God.

I will be with you (Isaac) and bless you.

I will give you and your descendants all these lands and confirm my oath with you (Isaac) that I swore to Abraham.

I will make your descendants as numerous as the stars in the sky.

Through your offspring, all the peoples of the earth will be blessed.

I will give you (Jacob) and your descendants the land on which you are lying.

Your descendants will be like the dust of the earth.

All peoples on earth will be blessed through you and your offspring.

I am with you and will watch over you wherever you go.

I will not leave you until I have done what I have promised you (Jacob).

Say to the group, **God's covenant with Abraham, which was reiterated to Isaac and Jacob, established the Hebrew nation. That nation ends up in Egypt through the provision of God through Joseph. A large portion of Genesis is devoted to Joseph (see Genesis 37—50). Joseph is the link between the family and the nation. God honored Joseph. There are at least 130 parallels between the life of Joseph and the life of Jesus. He is therefore the messianic patriarch, the patriarch who reflected Jesus Christ himself. Even as God redeemed Joseph from the pit and raised him to the pinnacle of power so God raised Jesus from the grave and exalted Him to the right hand of the Father. Also, in Joseph's life we can see a picture of how God through Jesus Christ redeems us from the pit of sin and death and raises us to new life in Jesus Christ.**

With the whole group, discuss the following:

How did God through the ages fulfill His covenant to Abraham?

How did God fulfill these promises through Jesus Christ?

How is God fulfilling these promises today in us as Christians?

SECTION TWO: GOD'S PERSON (15 MINUTES)

ABRAHAM: A MAN OF FAITH

Objective: To explore what it means to have faith in God, trusting Him as Abraham did.

Give everyone Session 3 handout, "Whom Do You Trust?" Give everyone a few minutes to complete their handouts through question two. With the whole group, list on a chalkboard, flipchart or overhead all the things they can see from Genesis 11 that Abraham knew about God when he left his home in Ur.

Now ask everyone to answer questions three through five on their handouts and to get back into their groups of two or three.

Ask the groups to share what they have written on their handouts and then discuss the following:

What would be the hardest thing to leave behind if you were asked like Abraham to leave where you live and go to a new place?

Would you have responded to God the way Abraham did? Why or why not? How hard is it to trust someone you do not know?

What would be more difficult for you in starting off a relationship with someone you did not know: faith, love or obedience? Why?

Finally, ask the small groups to complete questions six through eight. Ask the small groups to share their answers with one another and then to discuss **God asked Abraham to follow Him. Centuries later God calls us to follow Him in Jesus Christ. What is the hardest thing to leave behind when we trust and follow God?**

Say to the group, **A key element of God's Story is seen in Abraham.**

GOD ACTS AND SPEAKS FIRST—PEOPLE RESPOND

In small groups, ask each person to share:

What is the most difficult thing about trusting God?

Let's review the key elements of God's Story in Genesis.

1. **God created, people rebelled** (see Genesis 1:1; 3:6).
2. **God called, Abraham trusted** (see Hebrews 11:8-12,17-19).
3. **God sent Joseph and the rest of the family into Egypt, Israel securely waited on God there** (see Genesis 37—51).

(Have the group repeat those elements after you a few times)

Have everyone in the group share what they understand the word "covenant" to mean and write their statements on a chalkboard, flipchart or overhead.

Tell all group members to look at the end of their handouts and note the Bible readings for next week. Encourage everyone to do their readings before they return for the next session.

OPTION TWO: (FOR A 90-MINUTE SESSION)

Eight Names and Six Places in Genesis (15 Minutes)

Divide the whole group into three or more small groups. Give each group 14 3x5-inch cards. On a chalkboard, flipchart or overhead list the eight names of people in Genesis and six places of importance in the history of Genesis but scrambling the order of the lists. Have one member of each group write each person or location on a separate card. Instruct the groups to put the two lists in order, keeping the two sets of cards separate. See which group can put them in order first. When a group finishes and claims to have its two lists in the order they appear on the scene in Genesis, check the order. If both lists are ordered correctly then stop the process and give the right order to everyone in the group. Ask the group members to write these lists down on their handouts for future reference.

Eight Names	Six Places
God	Eden
Adam	Ararat
Satan	Babel
Noah	Ur of Chaldees
Abraham	Canaan
Isaac	Egypt
Jacob	
Joseph	

Now review as a group, each person with whom God made a covenant and what the covenant was.

SECTION THREE: GOD'S SON (10 MINUTES)

JESUS CHRIST REVEALED IN GENESIS

Objective: To explore ways that Jesus Christ can be seen in God's Story as revealed in Genesis.

Remember I mentioned the hope that God gave people in Genesis. This is the point in our study where we expand on that hope. How will God bless the peoples of the earth through Abraham?

Divide the whole group into four smaller groups. Give each group one of these passages—Matthew 1:1-17; Luke 1:67-75; John 8:50-59; Galatians 3:6-14—and ask them to answer this question:

How are Jesus and Abraham connected in God's Story based on this passage?

As a whole class, discuss that Jesus is also the hope given to Eve. Read Genesis 3:15. How did Jesus fulfill this hope?

The theme of one man is important throughout Genesis and all of the Bible. History pivoted on particular human beings in Genesis—Adam and Eve, Noah, Abraham, Isaac, Jacob and Joseph. Out of these individuals grew a family and then a nation. Out of that nation would come one Man through whom people would be saved. Often the history of our lives pivots on one person through whom we hear the Good News of salvation in Jesus Christ. Find a partner in your small group and share the name of one person who has played a very special part in your life in encouraging you to know Jesus Christ as Lord and Savior. Take about two minutes each to share.

Now discuss with the whole group:

Where do you see Jesus as the creative Word of God in Genesis (see John 1:1-3)?

How does Genesis reveal our need for a Savior and Redeemer?

What does Satan still do today that he did in Genesis?

How does sacrifice in Genesis point to the sacrifice of Jesus on the Cross?

PURSUING GOD (5 MINUTES)

NEXT STEPS I NEED TO TAKE

Objective: To take a realistic assessment of one's relationship with Jesus and how that relationship might grow closer in the coming week.

Ask the group members to pair up once again with the partners they had earlier. Ask them to share with one another.

One thing I learned about Jesus in this session was

_____.

One area in my relationship with Him that needs to grow is

_____.

The person in Genesis I identify most with in my spiritual walk right now is

_____.

My next step in walking closer with the Lord is

_____.

PRAYER (5 MINUTES)

SEEKING GOD'S GUIDANCE IN PRAYER

Objective: To close this session with affirmation and intercession in pairs.

Invite the pairs to encourage one another by saying, **One godly character quality I see in (name a person in Genesis) that I also see in you is**

_____.

You might give some examples like:

Abraham	Faith
Noah	Righteousness
Enoch	Close to God
Rachel	Love
Rebekah	Servanthood
Isaac	Obedience
Joseph	Integrity
Jacob	Persistence
Sarah	Desire to please her spouse
Melchizedek	Worshiper

Ask the prayer partners to share a prayer need with the other and then pray for one another.

One need that I have which studying Genesis has made me aware of is

_____.

Session 3 Bible *Tuck-In*™

UNDERSTANDING GENESIS

The purpose of this session is:

- To provide an overview of the book of Genesis;
- To discover how Jesus Christ is revealed in Genesis as our Creator-God.

KEY VERSES

"In the beginning God created the heavens and the earth." Genesis 1:1

"I will make you into a great nation and I will bless you; I will make your name great, and you will be a blessing. I will bless those who bless you, and whoever curses you I will curse; and all the peoples on earth will be blessed through you." Genesis 12:2,3

"In the beginning was the Word, and the Word was with God and the Word was God. He was with God in the beginning. Through him all things were made; without him nothing was made that has been made." John 1:1,2

SECTION ONE: GOD'S STORY (20 MINUTES)

GENESIS: BEGINNINGS

- Tell the group the Bible story, doing the suggested activities as

---------- Fold ----------

- Read Genesis 3:15. Discuss: **How did Jesus fulfill this hope?**
- As a whole group discuss the questions.

PURSUING GOD (5 MINUTES)

NEXT STEPS I NEED TO TAKE

- Ask the group members to pair up once again with the partners they had earlier. Ask them to share their completions for the following with one another.

One thing I learned about Jesus in this session was

_____

One area in my relationship with Him that needs to grow is

_____

The person in Genesis I identify most with in my spiritual walk right now is _____

My next step in walking closer with the Lord like Enoch is

_____

PRAYER (5 MINUTES)

SEEKING GOD'S GUIDANCE IN PRAYER

- Invite the pairs to encourage one another by saying,

One godly character quality I see in (name a person in Genesis) **that I also see in you is** _____

- Ask the prayer partners to share a prayer need with the other and then pray for one another.

One need that I have which studying Genesis has made me aware of is _____

you come to them. Distribute Session 3 handout, "An Overview of Genesis" so group members can take notes.

OPTION ONE: (FOR A 90-MINUTE SESSION)

The Patriarchal Period (15 Minutes)

• Divide the whole group into four small groups. Assign each small group one of the following passages: Genesis 12:1-3; 17:1-8; 26:1-5; 28:13-15. Make certain that every small group has pencil, paper and one person chosen to be the recorder. Ask each group to take two minutes to list all the promises made to Abraham by God in the passage they have been assigned.

• After two minutes for group members to read and summarize, invite someone to share a promise from the covenants. List the promises on a chalkboard, flipchart or overhead under the heading "God's Promises to Abraham." That list, when complete, would include a summary of this list from Genesis 12:1-3; 17:1-8; 26:1-5; 28:13-15.

• Discuss the questions.

SECTION TWO: GOD'S PERSON (20 MINUTES)

ABRAHAM: A MAN OF FAITH

• Give everyone Session 3 handout, "Whom Do You Trust?" Give everyone a few minutes to complete their handout through questions one and two. As a whole group, list on a chalkboard, flipchart or overhead all the things Abraham knew about God when he left his home in Ur.

• Ask everyone to answer questions three through five on their handouts and to get back into their groups of two or three.

• Discuss the questions.

• Ask the small groups to complete questions six through eight. Have

— Fold —

them share their answers with one another and then to discuss the questions.

• Review the key elements of God's story in Genesis.

• Tell all group members to look at the end of their handouts and note the Bible readings for next week. Encourage everyone to do their readings before they return for the next session.

OPTION TWO: (FOR A 90-MINUTE SESSION)

Eight Names and Six Places in Genesis (15 Minutes)

• Divide the whole group into three or more small groups. Give each group 14 3x5-inch cards. On a chalkboard, flipchart or overhead list the eight names of people in Genesis and six places of importance in the history of Genesis but scrambling the order of the lists. Have one member of each group write each person or location on a separate card. Instruct the groups to put the two lists in order, keeping the two sets of cards separate. See which group can put them in order first. When a group finishes and claims to have its two lists in the order they appear on the scene in Genesis, check the order. If both lists are ordered correctly then stop the process and give the right order to everyone in the group. Ask the group members to write these lists down on their handouts for future reference.

SECTION THREE: GOD'S SON (10 MINUTES)

JESUS CHRIST REVEALED IN GENESIS

• Divide the whole group into four smaller groups. Give each group one of these passages—Matthew 1:1-17; Luke 1:67-75; John 8:50-59; Galatians 3:6-14—and ask them to answer the question. **How are Jesus and Abraham connected in God's Story based on this passage?**

An Overview of Genesis

1. The Bible tells God's Story.

   Notes:

2. God created (see Genesis 1).

   Notes:

3. God created people in His image (see Genesis 1:26-28).

   Notes:

4. From the beginning, God desired and willed a relationship with people (see Genesis 2:1-25; 3:8).

   Notes:

5 God created; people rebelled—the Fall (see Genesis 3).

   Notes:

CONTINUED

6. God judges wickedness—the Flood (see Genesis 6—9).

   Notes:

7. God seeks people, but people cannot reach God by human effort (see Genesis 10).

   Notes:

8. God called; Abraham trusted (see Genesis 11—12).

   Notes:

9. Through Abraham, Isaac and Jacob, God made a covenant with a family to be His people (see Genesis 12;15; 17; 22; 26; 28).

   Notes:

10. From a family to a nation, God protected His people called Israel in the land of Egypt (see Genesis 37—50).

    Notes:

WHOM DO YOU TRUST?

1. Read Genesis 12:1—12:5 and Hebrews 11:8-10.

2. God sought out Abraham and Abraham trusted God. In this covenant relationship, God promised to bless Abraham and make of him and his descendants a great nation.

   List some of the likely barriers Abraham faced in trusting God.

   What are some likely reasons Abraham placed his trust in God?

3. Would it have been harder for Abraham to believe God about leaving his home and going to a strange land, or to believe the promise about his child? Why?

4. If you had been Abraham, what would have been the hardest part about trusting God?

5. Read Genesis 15:6. In a relationship with God, circle the one thing He expects of people.

Obedience	Humility	Love
Faith	Good Works	Righteousness

CONTINUED

Before next week, read the selected Bible readings.

Sunday: Bondage (Exodus 1:1-22)

Monday: The Call of Moses (Exodus 3—4)

Tuesday: The Plagues (Exodus 7:20—11:10)

Wednesday: The Passover (Exodus 12:1-51)

Thursday: The Law (Exodus 20:1-26)

Friday: The Worship (Exodus 25:1-9; 28:1-14,30-38)

Saturday: Moses' Commission Renewed (Exodus 33:12—34:17)

Understanding Exodus

The purpose of this session is:

- To provide an overview of the book of Exodus;
- To discover how Jesus Christ is revealed in Exodus as our Passover Lamb.

In this session, group members will learn:

- Key truths about God's story in the book of Exodus;
- That Jesus Christ is revealed in Exodus;
- The basic principle of redemption—how God sets His people free—redeeming them from bondage, slavery and death;
- How to apply basic truths to their own lives.

KEY VERSES

"God said to Moses, 'I AM WHO I AM. This is what you are to say to the Israelites: "I AM has sent me to you."'" Exodus 3:14

"God also said to Moses, 'I am the LORD. I appeared to Abraham, to Isaac and to Jacob as God Almighty, but by my name the LORD I did not make myself known to them. I also established my covenant with them to give them the land of Canaan, where they lived as aliens. Moreover, I have heard the groaning of the Israelites, whom the Egyptians are enslaving, and I have remembered my covenant.'" Exodus 6:2-5

BEFORE THE SESSION

- Pray for group members by name asking the Holy Spirit to teach them the spiritual truths in Exodus.
- Read chapter 3 in *What the Bible Is All About*.
- Prepare copies of Session 4 handouts, "An Overview of Exodus" and "The Ten Commandments and Me" for every group member.
- Check off these supplies once you have secured them:
  - ____ a $1 bill
  - ____ a red dry marker or completely washable paint or finger paint and paintbrush
- If you are having a 90-minute session, carefully read the two option sections right now and pull together any supplies you need for them.

- Read the entire session and look up every passage. Have your Bible *Tuck-In*™ ready for yourself.
- Arrive early and be ready to greet warmly each group member as he or she arrives.
- Memorize the key verse, Exodus 3:14 and become very familiar with the other key verses. Share them periodically in the session and ask the group to repeat the memorized verse after you.

SECTION ONE: GOD'S STORY (20 MINUTES)

EXODUS: THE WAY OUT

Objective: To tell how God sets His people free—redeeming them from bondage, slavery and death.

Explain to the group:

The book of Exodus means "way out" and today we are going to discover how God set His people free from slavery in Egypt. Nothing could redeem them—release or set them free from slavery in Egypt—except God. However, there were some things, like their food, which they desired to go back to even though they were not free in Egypt (see Exodus 16:3).

Read aloud the following, doing the suggested activities as you come to them. Distribute the handout "An Overview of Exodus" so group members can take notes.

God heard the cries of His people—Israel—who were slaves in Egypt (see Exodus 1).

Generations passed and the wonderful deeds of Joseph were forgotten by the present Pharaoh. He viewed the Hebrews as a threat. "They will join our enemies, fight us and leave the land" Pharaoh warned (see Exodus 1:10). Through slavery, Pharaoh forced the Hebrews to construct buildings and to labor in the fields. Pharaoh ordered all male Hebrew babies to be slaughtered.

As a group, discuss:

What views of God would you expect the Hebrews to have at this time?
What response from God do you think the Hebrews desired?

God prepared and then called Moses to lead His people to freedom (see Exodus 2—4).

One Hebrew mother hid her baby boy in reeds along the banks of the Nile River.

He was discovered by an Egyptian princess and raised as her own. At about the age of forty, this Egyptian prince named Moses saw an Egyptian beating a Hebrew slave; he killed the Egyptian and fled to the Midian wilderness. There Moses married Jethro's daughter Zipporah and dwelled there forty years tending sheep. Around the age of 80, he saw a bush burning without being consumed. Curious, he approached the bush—from which God spoke to him. The call and command of God was simple: Go to Egypt and lead the Hebrews to freedom. No excuse that Moses offered changed the call or the command of God. God sent Moses back to Egypt for a confrontation with Pharaoh.

Relate this quote by D.L. Moody to your class:

"Moses spent
Forty years thinking he was somebody;
Forty years learning he was nobody;
Forty years discovering what God can do with nobody."

As a whole group discuss:
Who are some other people in the Bible that God used many years to prepare before they could serve Him? (That list might include David, Jesus, Ruth, Peter and Paul.)

Pharaoh's hardened heart could not understand or obey God's command resulting in plagues and death coming upon him and his people (see Exodus 5—10).

The 10 plagues God sent on Egypt gave a message to Pharaoh and the Egyptians that God was more powerful than all their beliefs or gods, including Pharaoh and the River Nile that they worshiped.

Take out a $1 bill. Discuss as a class:
How would you feel if I tore up the $1 bill?
How would you feel if I tore up a $5, $10, $20, $50 or $100 bill?
Would your feelings change with the larger bills?
How is money like a powerful idol in our culture?
If someone came into our society and destroyed all money, how would they be received?
Through Moses, God destroyed the most precious and powerful idols in the Egyptian culture. How do you suppose Pharaoh and the Egyptians treated Moses? Why didn't Pharaoh change his mind?

The blood of the Passover lamb redeeming God's people from death (the last plague) provides a historical picture of Jesus Christ—the Lamb of God—Who redeems us from sin and death (see Exodus 11—12).

Jesus is seen powerfully in Exodus. "Exodus" in Greek, means "way out." Jesus

declares in the Gospel of John, "I am the way and the truth and the life. No one comes to the Father except through me.... If you hold to my teaching, you are really my disciples. Then you will know the truth, and the truth will set you free" (John 14:6; 8:31,32). John the Baptist said, "Look, the Lamb of God, who takes away the sin of the world"—a clear allusion to Christ as the Passover Lamb (John 1:29).

Take a dry erase marker that you would use on a white board, or any type of non-permanent marker, or finger paint that can be easily wiped or washed from the doorposts of your room. Walk over to the doorpost and mark or paint a cross on both sides and the top. Tell the group that you are putting the blood of the lamb on the doorposts and that if it were real blood, it would also be dripping down onto the threshold as well. Ask the group members to share what they see. Include in your discussion that the shape of the cross is being made and that Jesus refers to Himself as the Door or Gate (see John 10:7; 1 Corinthians 5:7).

Jesus took this Passover meal and remade it into the Lord's Supper. The Israelites had to make unleavened bread and eat it since they had no time to let the bread rise. Jesus took the unleavened bread of Passover and called it His Body. The wine of Passover, He called His Blood.

OPTION ONE: (FOR A 90-MINUTE SESSION)

Passover and the Lord's Supper (15 Minutes)

Say to the group: **Exodus 12 gives us the thrilling story of the Passover, the clearest Old Testament picture of our individual salvation through faith in the shed blood of our Lord Jesus Christ. This chapter is the basis for calling Christ the Lamb of God, Christ our Passover and the many tender references to His crucifixion as the death of our own Passover Lamb. "For Christ, our Passover lamb, has been sacrificed" (1 Corinthians 5:7).**

Have the elements of communion—unleavened bread and wine or grape juice prepared. If required in your church, have the pastor or an elder preside. Ask each person to hold in his or her hands the elements and meditate on them as you describe the divine order of Passover as given in Exodus 12. After partaking of communion, assign various group members these passages and be ready to read when you call out each Scripture reference: Hebrews 9:28; Isaiah 53:6; John 19:14; 1 Corinthians 5:7; Hebrews 9:22; 1 John 1:7; Revelation 1:5; John 1:12; John 5:54-58; Psalm 139:23,24; Hebrews 12:11; Psalm 34:20; John 19:36.

In celebrating the first Passover, the Hebrews:

1. Took a Lamb: (see Hebrews 9:28; Isaiah 53:6; John 19:14; 1 Corinthians 5:7). It was not the spotlessness of the living lamb that saved them (see Hebrews 9:22; 1 John 1:7; Revelation 1:5). It was not Christ's sinless life that saved us, but His death on the cross.

2. Sprinkled the blood. It is not enough for the lamb to be slain. The blood was sufficient but not efficient unless applied. Every Israelite individually had to apply the blood to his own household on the doorposts. What have you done with the blood, the blood of our Passover Lamb who died on Calvary (see John 1:12)? The hyssop—a common weed but obtainable by everyone—typical of faith. The blood on the lintel is that which saved; not what they thought about, but what they did with it counted. "When I see the blood, I will pass over you" (Exodus 12:13).

3. Ate the Lamb. After the blood was shed and sprinkled, then there was a direction for nourishment, etc. So with us: salvation, first, then feeding—fellowship, worship, walk and service. Feeding did not save them, but blood first; then nourishment was possible (see John 6:54-58).

4. Removed the yeast. Read Psalm 139:23,24. Leaven represents sin (see Matthew 16:6 and 1 Corinthians 5:7). The leaven of unrighteousness must be removed from our lives if we are to eat with God.

5. Tasted bitter herbs. Christ tasted the bitter cup for us and we, too, must taste some bitterness—suffer (see Hebrews 12:11). The lamb to be feasted upon not raw, not unbaked, but a suffering lamb who passed through fire. Nothing was to be left—eaten in haste and nothing remaining. Not a bone broken! Christ's body was broken but not His bones (see Psalm 34:20; John 19:36).

6. Were prepared to leave. They ate the food standing, fully dressed, ready to go. All provision was made for the journey. What a contrast that night! Peaceful feasting in the houses of Israel; awful mourning in the houses of Egypt!

As a group discuss:

What meaning does studying the first Passover give to you as you partake of the Lord's Supper?

God redeemed Israel by parting the Red Sea and preserving them in the wilderness (see Exodus 13—18).

Even after the terrible tenth plague which caused Pharaoh to let them leave Egypt, Moses and the people still feared Pharaoh as they stood on the banks of the Red Sea.

Moses and the Israelites stood on the banks of the Red Sea with Pharaoh's army quickly closing in behind them. Even Moses was afraid. God commanded Moses to stretch out his hand over the sea and a mighty wind sent from God separated the sea, providing dry land for the Israelites to cross over to the other side.

After Israel passed through the Red Sea on dry land and was safely on the

other side, Pharaoh's army in hot pursuit was drowned as the sea closed over them. And God's mighty acts of deliverance and provision continued when the people found themselves without food or water in the wilderness.

God revealed His law to Moses on Mount Sinai (see Exodus 19—31).

God led Israel with a pillar of fire by night and a cloud by day through the wilderness to Mount Sinai. There He sought to meet with His people as the mountain shook with thunder and smoked with fire. Afraid, the Israelites asked Moses to meet with God on their behalf. Moses climbed the mountain, met with God and received the Ten Commandments on stone tablets. In the meantime, Aaron gave into the people's demands to worship as the Egyptians did and constructed a golden calf. Moses descended from meeting with God to see the Israelites worshiping an idol. In anger, he threw down the stone tablets breaking them into pieces.

Without Moses' leadership, the Israelites reverted to worshiping idols and desiring to return to Egypt, slavery and bondage (see Exodus 32—34).

People are fickle. Without Moses, they stray back to their old idols and bondages.
    As a class discuss:

What can keep us from straying back into sin like the Israelites did? (In this discussion, be certain to mention the convicting and sanctifying work of the Holy Spirit in our lives, the power of prayer, the encouragement and strength we have as the Body of Christ to help one another overcome temptations, and the Word of God.)

God provided the Tabernacle for His people to see His presence and worship Him (see Exodus 35—40).

Tell the group: **Look at your handout, "The Tabernacle." As I mention each part of the Tabernacle, label it and make any notes necessary to remember how it reminds us of Jesus.** God told Moses He wanted a sanctuary, a dwelling place—a tabernacle—which pointed to Christ and told of His person and work as we read in the book of Hebrews. Here is how the Tabernacle represented Christ.

- The Gate—Every Hebrew had to enter the Tabernacle by a single outer gate (see Exodus 38:18). Jesus Christ is the only way to God and is Himself the gate (see John 14 and 10).
- The Outer Court—Here we see the brazen altar on which the burnt offerings were sacrificed. Remember, Christ is our sin offering (see Exodus 27:1-8). The laver was here for the cleansing of the priest before he could enter into the holy place to render his service (see Exodus 30:18).
- The Holy Place—Herein was the golden lampstand (see Exodus 25:31-40) typifying Christ as the Light of the world, and the bread of the Presence (see Exodus 25:23-30) representing Christ as the Bread of Life, and the golden

Session
4

altar of incense (see Exodus 30:1-10) symbolizing Christ's intercession for us.

- **The Holy of Holies**—Now if we draw back the beautiful veil (which typifies the body of Christ), we will see the Ark of the Covenant, the symbol of God's presence. Into this holy of holies, the high priest came only once a year to sprinkle the blood of atonement. The book of Hebrews tells us that Christ is not only our High Priest, but that He also is our atonement, so we can go with boldness into the holy of holies (the presence of God) at any time.

- **The Tabernacle**—With the cloud of glory over it, taught the people that God was dwelling in their midst (see Exodus 25:8). Since God's Spirit indwells us as believers, we are now the tabernacle of God in our day (see 1 Corinthians 3).

Send the group members back into their groups of three or four. Ask them to share with one another:

What is one thing you learned about the Tabernacle that teaches you about your relationship with Jesus Christ?

SECTION TWO: GOD'S PERSON (20 MINUTES)

MOSES: A MAN OF OBEDIENCE

Objective: To learn from Moses how we can follow and obey God's calling in our lives.

Ask everyone to get into their small groups of three or four. Ask each group to select a secretary and a reader. Assign Exodus 3:1-14 and 4:1-17 to every group. Have the readers read their passages to their small groups. Have everyone in the small group listen for the excuses that Moses made for *not* obeying God. Have the secretary write down these excuses. Give the groups about 10 minutes to do this.

After 10 minutes, ask the groups to spend another two minutes listing all of the excuses we make to God for not obeying Him.

Bring the whole group back together. Ask all the secretaries to report what they have on their two lists. Record these lists on a chalkboard, flipchart or overhead.

Now ask the group:

Why do you suppose that God chose Moses? (Later we learn that Moses was meek and humble; perhaps his faith grew greatly when he was in the wilderness.)

63

Why was it so difficult for Moses to accept God's call and command to go back to Egypt? (Perhaps he feared Pharaoh and his own people; or he lacked courage; or he thought he was too old; or he simply feared the possibility of death.)

What qualities did Moses exhibit in Egypt and before Israel as a leader that seem lacking in this story? (For example, Moses had boldness, courage, forceful speech and miraculous power through God that he didn't seem to have in the wilderness before he returned to Egypt.)

Why are we reluctant to obey God today?

What can we learn from Moses?

If God could use Moses, can He use us?

OPTION TWO: (FOR A 90-MINUTE SESSION)

The Ten Commandments and Me (15 Minutes)

Divide the group into groups of three or four. Ask each person to complete Session 4 handout, "The Ten Commandments and Me." After everyone has completed the handout, invite them to share with their small groups the one commandment that's easiest to keep and one of the commandments that they see significant growth in obeying over the last 10 years.

After the small groups have finished, assign each group two or three of the Ten Commandments so each is covered. Have them paraphrase their commandments in contemporary language. Write the groups' paraphrases on a chalkboard, flipchart or overhead.

SECTION THREE: GOD'S SON (10 MINUTES)

JESUS CHRIST REVEALED IN EXODUS

Objective: To discover how Jesus Christ is revealed in Exodus.

Remember our discussion of the Tabernacle (and the Lord's Supper if you did that as a group). **Jesus Christ is revealed in Exodus through the Passover, the Tabernacle and the Commandments of God. In your small groups, discuss and seek to uncover at least three ways you can see Jesus revealed in Exodus.**

Give the small groups about three minutes to discuss this and then bring the whole group back together and ask the groups to share what they have uncovered. Among those things that are shared, the following three critical points need to be made. Write them on a chalkboard, flipchart or overhead for the group and invite everyone to write these points down on their handouts.

1. Jesus Christ is the "Exodus" or "The Way out" of sin and bondage to freedom, abundant and eternal life.
2. Jesus Christ is the sinless, perfect Lamb of God, who is our Passover Lamb shedding His blood for our redemption from sin.
3. Jesus Christ is our High Priest in the heavenly tabernacle making continual intercession for us.

PURSUING GOD (5 MINUTES)

NEXT STEPS I NEED TO TAKE

Objective: To take a realistic assessment of one's relationship with Jesus and how that relationship might grow closer in the coming week.

Ask the group members to think about this list and to choose one way they need to grow more in their relationship with Christ. Read through the following list slowly and maybe even twice so that the group members can chose one of the things on the list:

To be more obedient to the Lord in obeying the Ten Commandments.

To listen more carefully to God's voice.

To stop making excuses to God for why I cannot obey Him.

To grow in my worship of Him through the Lord's Supper—remembering Passover.

To take more seriously the power of the blood of Jesus Christ and His redeeming me from sin.

To be more willing to leave the "bondages" of Egypt behind me.

To risk the liberty of God's future over the comfort and bondage of Egypt's past.

To obey God's call in my life.

To become the kind of servant Moses was so that God may use me.

Invite everyone to find a partner and to share with that partner one way that they need to be more obedient to the Lord in the coming week. Have the partners pray with one another after they have shared.

PRAYER (5 MINUTES)

SEEKING GOD'S GUIDANCE IN PRAYER

Objective: To close this session with a deeper commitment to obeying God.

Have the whole group form a circle. Invite each person to close this session by praying their own completion to this sentence prayer:

Jesus, like Moses I desire to obey your call for me to _____.

Session 4 Bible *Tuck-In*™

UNDERSTANDING EXODUS

The purpose of this session is:

- To provide an overview of the book of Exodus;
- To discover how Jesus Christ is revealed in Exodus as our Passover Lamb.

KEY VERSES

"God said to Moses, 'I AM WHO I AM. This is what you are to say to the Israelites: "I AM has sent me to you."'" Exodus 3:14

"God also said to Moses, 'I am the LORD. I appeared to Abraham, to Isaac and to Jacob as God Almighty, but by my name the LORD I did not make myself known to them. I also established my covenant with them to give them the land of Canaan, where they lived as aliens. Moreover, I have heard the groaning of the Israelites, whom the Egyptians are enslaving, and I have remembered my covenant.'" Exodus 6:2-5

SECTION ONE: GOD'S STORY (20 MINUTES)

EXODUS: THE WAY OUT

- Tell the group the Bible story doing the suggested activities as you come to them. Distribute the handout "An Overview of Exodus" so group members can take notes.

PURSUING GOD (5 MINUTES)

NEXT STEPS I NEED TO TAKE

- Read through the following list slowly and maybe even twice so that the group members can choose one of the ways they need to grow in their relationship with Christ.

To be more obedient to the Lord in obeying the Ten Commandments

To listen more carefully to God's voice.

To stop making excuses to God for why I cannot obey Him.

To grow in my worship of Him through the Lord's Supper remembering Passover.

To take more seriously the power of the blood of Jesus Christ and His redeeming me from sin.

To be more willing to leave the "bondages of Egypt" behind me.

To risk the liberty of God's future over the comfort of Egypt's past.

To obey God's call in my life.

To become the kind of servant Moses was so that God may use me.

- Invite everyone to find a partner and to share with that partner one way that they need to be more obedient to the Lord in the coming week. Have the partners pray with one another after they have shared.

PRAYER (5 MINUTES)

SEEKING GOD'S GUIDANCE IN PRAYER

- Have the whole group form a circle. Invite each person to close this group session, by praying their own completion to this sentence prayer:

Jesus, like Moses I desire to obey your call for me to _____ .

OPTION ONE: (FOR A 90-MINUTE SESSION)

Passover and the Lord's Supper (15 Minutes)

- Say to the group: Exodus 12 gives us the thrilling story of the Passover, the clearest Old Testament picture of our individual salvation through faith in the shed blood of our Lord Jesus Christ. This chapter is the basis for calling Christ the Lamb of God, Christ our Passover, and the many tender references to His crucifixion as the death of our own Passover lamb. "For Christ, our Passover lamb, has been sacrificed" (1 Corinthians 5:7).

- Have the elements of communion.

- After partaking of communion, assign various group members these passages and be ready to read when you call out each Scripture reference: Hebrews 9:28; 1 John 1:7; Revelation 1:5; John 1:12; John 6:54-58; Psalm 139:23,24; Hebrews 12:11; Psalm 34:20; Corinthians 5:7; Hebrews 9:22; 1 John 1:7; Isaiah 53:6; John 19:14; 1 John 19:36.

- Review with the group the meaning of Passover and how it portrays Jesus Christ.

SECTION TWO: GOD'S PERSON (20 MINUTES)

MOSES: A MAN OF OBEDIENCE

- In groups of three or four, assign Exodus 3:1-14 and 4:1-17 to every group. Have the readers read their passages to their small groups and another person record all the excuses the group can think of that Moses made and we make *not* to obey God.

- After sharing the Moses list and their lists of excuses, discuss the questions provided.

- - - - - - Fold - - - - - -

OPTION TWO: (FOR A 90-MINUTE SESSION)

The Ten Commandments and Me (15 Minutes)

- Give everyone the handout on the Ten Commandments and ask them to complete it. Then invite the small groups to share the easiest ones to keep and the ones in which they have grown the most in the last 10 years.

- After the small groups have finished, assign each group two or three of the Ten Commandments so each is covered. Have them paraphrase their commandments in contemporary language. Write the groups' paraphrases on a chalkboard, flipchart or overhead.

SECTION THREE: GOD'S SON (10 MINUTES)

JESUS CHRIST REVEALED IN EXODUS

- In small groups, ask the group members to share at least three ways they can see Jesus Christ revealed in Exodus.

- When the groups have finished their sharing, have them share their findings with the total group. Then have them summarize and write down these three points:

1. Jesus Christ is the Exodus or the Way out of sin and bondage to freedom, abundant and eternal life.

2. Jesus Christ is the sinless, perfect Lamb of God, who is our Passover Lamb shedding His blood for our redemption from sin.

3. Jesus Christ is our High Priest in the heavenly tabernacle making continual intercession for us.

An Overview of Exodus

1. God heard the cries of His people—Israel—who were slaves in Egypt (see Exodus 1).

   Notes:

2. God prepared and then called Moses to lead His people to freedom (see Exodus 2—4).

   Notes:

3. Pharaoh's hardened heart cannot understand or obey God's command resulting in plagues and death coming upon him and his people (see Exodus 5—10).

   Notes:

4. The blood of the Passover lamb redeeming God's people from death (the last plague) provides a historical picture of Jesus Christ—the Lamb of God—Who redeems us from sin and death (see Exodus 11—12).

   Notes:

5. God redeemed Israel by parting the Red Sea and preserving the people in the wilderness (see Exodus 13—18).

   Notes:

6. God revealed His Law to Moses on Mount Sinai (see Exodus 19—31).

   Notes:

7. Without Moses' leadership, the Israelites reverted back to worshiping idols and desiring to return to Egypt, slavery and bondage (see Exodus 32—34).

   Notes:

8. God provided the Tabernacle for His people to see His presence and worship Him (see Exodus 35—40)

   Notes:

THE TABERNACLE

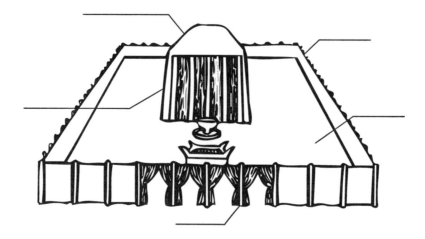

CONTINUED

In Exodus, three ways Jesus Christ is revealed are:

1.

2.

3.

Before next week's session, read:
Monday: The Priests (Leviticus 8); The Report of the Spies (Numbers 13:16-33)
Tuesday: Pure Food Laws (Leviticus 11); Israel's Unbelief (Numbers 20:1-13)
Wednesday: The Day of Atonement (Leviticus 16); Water from the Rock (Numbers 21:1-9)
Thursday: The Feasts of Jehovah (Leviticus 23); The Brazen Serpent (Numbers 21:1-9)
Friday: God's Pledge (Leviticus 26); The Cities of Refuge (Numbers 35:6-34)
Saturday: Dedication (Leviticus 27)

THE TEN COMMANDMENTS AND ME

Read each scale based on one of the Ten Commandments. Put an *x* on the line where you are right now and an *O* on the line where you were 10 years ago. Listen for your group leader's instructions on how to share.

"I am the Lord your God, who brought you out of Egypt, out of the land of slavery. You shall have no other gods before me" (Exodus 20:2,3).

I have no other gods.	I sometimes worship the God I want rather than the God Who is the I AM.	I let stuff or people come between me and God.

"You shall not make for yourself an idol in the form of anything in heaven above or on the earth beneath or in the waters below. You shall not bow down to them or worship them; for I, the Lord your God, am a jealous God" (Exodus 20:4,5).

I have no idols.	At times, I make idols of other people, stuff or my work.	I worship the things of this world.

"You shall not misuse the name of the Lord your God, for the Lord will not hold anyone guiltless who misuses his name" (Exodus 20:7).

I never misuse God's name.	I sometimes misuse His Name.	I often misuse God's name.

"Remember the Sabbath day by keeping it holy. Six days you shall labor and do all your work, but the seventh day is a Sabbath" (Exodus 20:8-10).

I observe a Sabbath.	I partially keep a Sabbath but use the rest of the time for myself.	I work or play all the time.

"Honor your father and mother" (Exodus 20:12).

I honor my parents.	I do not honor my parents.

CONTINUED

"You shall not murder" (Exodus 20:13).

| I do not murder. | I don't kill but I hate at times. | I have killed or I hate persons. |

"You shall not commit adultery" (Exodus 20:14).

| I do not commit adultery. | At times I lust. | I lust or commit adultery. |

"You shall not steal" (Exodus 20:15).

| I do not steal. | At times I steal. | I steal. |

"You shall not give false testimony against your neighbor" (Exodus 20:16).

| I do not lie. | I lie sometimes. | I lie often. |

"You shall not covet" (Exodus 20:17).

| I covet no person or thing. | I covet sometimes. | I covet often. |

Understanding Leviticus and Numbers

The purpose of this session is:

- To provide an overview of the books of Leviticus and Numbers;
- To discover how Jesus Christ is portrayed in the book of Leviticus as our Sacrifice for sin and in Numbers as our "Lifted-Up One."

In this session, group members will learn:

- Key truths about God's story in the books of Leviticus and Numbers;
- That Jesus Christ is revealed in the books of Leviticus and Numbers;
- The basic principles of worship—how to present sacrifices and offerings, showing dependence upon God;
- How to apply basic truths in their own lives.

KEY VERSES

"I am the Lord who brought you up out of Egypt to be your God; therefore be holy, because I am holy." Leviticus 11:45

"The cloud of the Lord was over them by day when they set out from the camp. Whenever the ark set out, Moses said, 'Rise up, O Lord! May your enemies be scattered; may your foes flee before you.' Whenever it came to rest, he said, 'Return, O Lord, to the countless thousands of Israel.'" Numbers 10:34-36

"Now the people complained about their hardships in the hearing of the Lord, and when he heard them his anger was aroused." Numbers 11:1

BEFORE THE SESSION

- Pray for group members by name asking the Holy Spirit to teach them the spiritual truths in these two books.
- Read chapters 4 and 5 in *What the Bible Is All About*.
- Prepare copies of Session 5 handouts, "An Overview of Leviticus and Numbers" and, "Content or Complaining" for every group member.

- Check off these supplies once you have secured them:

   ____ M&Ms™ or unwrapped hard candy and a cup or bag to contain them.

   ____ Catsup and oil

   ____ A bowl of water and towel or paper towels

   ____ Write the following chart on a chalkboard, flipchart or overhead before the session.

   The Feast of the Sabbath (See Leviticus 23:1-3)

   The Feast of the Passover (See Leviticus 23:4,5)

   The Feast of Pentecost (See Leviticus 23:15-22)

   The Feast of Trumpets (See Leviticus 23:23-25)

   The Day of Atonement (See Leviticus 23:26-32)

   The Feast of Tabernacles (See Leviticus 23:33-36)

   The Sabbatical Year (See Leviticus 25:1-7)

   The Year of Jubilee (See Leviticus 25:8-24)

- If you are having a 90-minute session, then carefully read the two option sections right now and pull together any supplies you need for them.

- Read the entire session and look up every passage. Have your Bible *Tuck-In*™ ready for yourself.

- Arrive early and be ready to warmly greet each group member as he or she arrives.

- Memorize the key verses. Share them periodically in the session and ask the group to repeat them after you.

SECTION ONE: GOD'S STORY (25 MINUTES)

On a chalkboard, flipchart or overhead write the word "worship" vertically. Have group members add words that relate to worship that contain a letter contained in worship.

wonder
o
glory
s
h
i
p

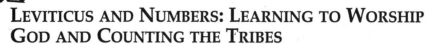

LEVITICUS AND NUMBERS: LEARNING TO WORSHIP GOD AND COUNTING THE TRIBES

Objective: To tell God's story in Leviticus and Numbers so that the group members will understand how God desired a holy people who would worship and serve Him no matter what the circumstance or situation.

Read aloud the following, doing the suggested activities as you come to them. Distribute the handout "An Overview of Leviticus and Numbers" so group members can take notes.

God revealed a pattern of worship to Israel.

God gave Israel *Offerings* to remind them to "Get right." He gave *Feasts* to remind them to "Keep right." He gave a system of *Sacrifice* which emphasized blood atonement—the covering of sin through blood sacrifice.

> **In Genesis we see humanity ruined.**
> **In Exodus, humanity redeemed.**
> **In Leviticus, humanity worshiping.**
> **In Numbers, humanity serving.**

Take some M&Ms (or other small candies) and throw them out, scattering them on the floor. Lightly step on some and ask the class members to help you collect them into a paper cup or bag. Now ask the ones in the class who would *not* want to eat these M&Ms to stand. Ask them to share why they wouldn't eat them and then to be seated. The main reason some will not eat the candy is that it is unclean. Point out that our natural reluctance to eat the candy because it's not clean gives us a glimmer of understanding of why God will never accept any unclean thing.

God who is holy and pure demands a people who are holy and pure (see Leviticus 1—5).

Throughout Leviticus, God demands that His people are to be holy even as He is holy (see Leviticus 20:7, compare with 1 Peter 1:16 and Matthew 5:48). Holiness means to be pure and separated, completely devoted to God. All the sacrifices of this book point to the Lamb of God, who takes away the sin of the world (see John 1:29). Since "the wages of sin is death" (Romans 6:23), there can be no fellowship with God until sin has been dealt with and the only way is through blood sacrifice. "Without the shedding of blood there is no forgiveness" (Hebrews 9:22).

Divide your class into five small groups. Assign each group a sacrifice. Instruct them to look up and skim the passage associated with that sacrifice. Then they are to bring a summary of their discussion back to share with the whole group:

> The Burnt Offering (See Leviticus 1)
> The Meal Offering (See Leviticus 2)
> The Peace Offering (See Leviticus 3)

The Sin Offering (See Leviticus 4—5:13)

The Trespass Offering (See Leviticus 5:14—6:7)

After about five minutes, bring the groups back together and have them share what they discussed. Then instruct them to write down these notes on their handouts.

The Burnt Offering pictures the _surrender_ of Jesus for the world.

The Meal Offering pictures the _service_ of Christ in life.

The Peace Offering pictures the _serenity_ of Christ in life.

The Sin Offering pictures the _substitute_ of Christ for sin.

The Trespass Offering pictures the _satisfaction_ by Christ for the demands of God.

The priests of the tribe of Levi presented to God the sacrifices, prayers and praises of God's people (see Leviticus 6—10; Numbers 3)

Priests presided over the worship of Israel. Bringing his animal for sacrifice, the burdened Israelite laid his hands on the head of the animal which was then sacrificed and its blood sprinkled on the altar. Representing the worshiper, the priest then came to the laver, in which he washed his hands indicating the clean life that should follow the forgiveness of sins.

Once a year on the Day of Atonement, the High Priest went into the holy of holies to sprinkle blood on the mercy seat of the ark atoning for the sins of Israel.

Ask for a male volunteer to come in front of the group. Announce that this man is a Levite and is about to be consecrated as a priest. Take a bowl of water and ask the man to wash his hands. Take some oil and pour a small amount on his head. Take some blood (catsup) in a cup and take your index finger dipping into the "blood." Touch the "blood" to the man's right ear lobe, right thumb and right toe. Explain to the group that Aaron and his sons were consecrated as priests before the Lord through the blood covering, or atonement. They were made holy through the blood. The only way to enter God's presence was to be consecrated as holy before God. Say, **The priests were consecrated by washing which represented the cleansing of the heart to serve God; by anointing with oil which represented the outpouring of God's Spirit on the priest and the complete bodily consecration represented by the blood. The priest's hearing and understanding, the work of his hands and the walk of his life were devoted fully to God.**

The Holiness Code formed the basis for the Israelite community (see Leviticus 11—27; Numbers 15; 18—29).

In His project to create a people for Himself, God gave Moses a comprehensive body of laws, sometimes called the "Holiness Code." God wanted to mold His people into a showcase people: a holy, distinct people, who could in turn share that holiness and blessing with the surrounding idol-worshiping peoples.

Three types of laws were contained in the Holiness Code: moral laws such as

the Ten Commandments; civil laws dealing with property, personal injury and crimes against the community; and ceremonial laws describing which things and activities were "clean" and "unclean." Combined with the ritual (sacrificial) laws, the law of Moses was intended to teach the Israelites—and the surrounding peoples—about the character of the One True God, to test their obedience to His commands, and to bless them with health and peace. According to the Apostle Paul, the law was also intended to lead the people to Christ (see Galatians 3:24).

The five sacrificial offerings spoke of the blood that atoned for sin. The eight feasts spoke of the food that sustained. Both are of God (see Leviticus 11—27; Numbers 15; 18—19; 28—29).

Divide the whole group into eight groups. Refer to the feasts you listed on the chalkboard, flipchart or overhead. Assign each group one of the following feasts. Have each group read the passage of that feast and discuss what the feast reminds us to be thankful that God provides.

After about five minutes, have the whole group share what they discovered.

As Israel left Mount Sinai, God provided for their needs and prepared them to enter the Promised Land of Canaan (see Numbers 9—12).

Starting with Numbers 9:15, God led Israel through the wilderness with a cloud by day and pillar of fire by night. He provided manna, quail and water for physical needs while clothing them with garments and shoes that would not wear out. But the Hebrews who had witnessed God open the Red Sea, drown Pharaoh's army, defeat enemies along the way, miraculously provide for all their needs, give them the Law and the way to worship Him are the same people who complained about everything. After a year they arrive at Paran, the southern border of the Promised Land. Are they prepared to enter and possess the land?

After sending twelve spies into Canaan, Israel learned there were giants in the land. Only Caleb and Joshua urged going forward and possessing the land (see Numbers 13).

God was angered as Israel rebelled and refused to enter the Promised Land. God declared that the entire generation would perish in the wilderness except for Joshua and Caleb.

Have everyone find a partner. Ask them to fill out Session 5 handout, "Content or Complaining?" Instruct the partners to share their answers to the questions at the bottom of the page and then to pray for one another. Give them five minutes to complete this.

Moses disobeyed God by striking a rock in anger to get water for the people. Both Israel and Moses failed God's test of faithfully obeying

and trusting His leading (see Numbers 14—36).

The test of the wilderness is to trust God no matter what the circumstance or trial. As Israel moved on to Canaan, they continued to complain and murmur. They were attacked by serpents. Looking upon a brass serpent lifted up on a pole delivered the Hebrews just as Jesus lifted up on the cross defeats death and Satan, delivering us from a curse to eternal life (see John 3:14; Numbers 21:9).

OPTION ONE: (FOR A 90-MINUTE SESSION)

The Burnt Offering (15 Minutes)

Say, **The offerings start with the burnt offering and end with the trespass offering. The burnt offering is a symbol of Christ offering Himself without blemish to God. There were daily burnt offerings. This was an offering of dedication. Why was this first? Because sacrifice comes first. No one begins with God until he has yielded all. This was the most common sacrifice in the ancient Tabernacle and Temple.**

Let's focus on this one offering.

Make a list of everything the group suggests. Then as a group, choose the three most difficult things to surrender.

Divide the group into pairs. Invite them to share with their partners what the most difficult thing to surrender as a burnt offering to the Lord is or has been in their lives (see Romans 12:1,2). Have them pray for each other. Then gather the group back together.

Say, **Our burnt offering is to sacrifice all we are and have to the Lord.**

SECTION TWO: GOD'S PERSON (15 MINUTES)

JOSHUA AND CALEB: WILLING TO TRUST GOD AND POSSESS THE LAND

Objective: To understand from the example of Joshua and Caleb how we can face life's giants with confidence and boldness in the Lord.

Briefly summarize the story of the 12 spies found in Numbers 13. Write these two headings on a chalkboard, flipchart or overhead.

    Joshua and Caleb   The Other Spies

Suggest and list the attitudes and qualities of Joshua and Caleb and the attitudes and qualities of the other spies.

Invite those who wish to share with the whole group about a time in their lives when they faced "giants in the land." Ask for a show of hands of those who ever let a big problem keep them from doing what they felt God wanted. Give an example from your own life. Request that some share an example. Request that others share how God helped them defeat a giant in their lives. Take time to hear three or four testimonies in these areas.

Say, **We learn from both the victories and wilderness experiences in our lives. Of course, it's far more exciting and pleasant to experience victory—but we must be willing to risk and to trust God completely. God wins the battles and defeats the enemy. We cannot face giants in our own strength. Like Israel, we also learn from wandering in the wilderness though it may be painful and filled with suffering. Think of it. At Kadesh, Israel was only eleven days from the land of promise, but they turned back! They could have made eleven days of progress, but they chose forty years of wandering. God opens doors and no man closes, and He closes doors and no man opens (see Isaiah 22:22 and Revelation 3:8). God did not want the children of Israel just to come out of Egypt. He wanted to have them come into the Promised Land. As we have seen, their fear disqualified them from taking over the land of promise. Oftentimes it is our fear that keeps us from enjoying all that God wants to give us. We fear what others will say. We fear what might happen if we put our trust completely in Christ.**

OPTION TWO: (FOR A 90-MINUTE SESSION)

The Wilderness Experience (15 Minutes)

Divide the group into three smaller groups. Share with them that they are going to be living in a desert wilderness for at least one year. Each group is to choose only five things that they can take into the wilderness with them for survival. They may not take any twentieth-century stuff. They may only take what the Hebrews might have had with them in Egypt as slaves.

Give every group five minutes to make up a list of things they will take into the wilderness. Bring everyone back together to share their lists. As the leader, make a master list of all the items on a chalkboard, flipchart or overhead.

With the whole group, eliminate taking anything that will perish soon after the journey begins. Ask, **What three things does the group believe they need which would be essential for survival?** It may be difficult for the group to identify anything that will last on a long wilderness journey. That's just the point. Nothing we have or are will endure the journey through the wilderness. All that lasts must come from the God who has it all and sustains it all.

Divide into three groups (mothers, fathers and children) and assign each of the three groups a set of 12 chapters from Numbers:

> Group One (Numbers 1—12);
> Group Two (Numbers 13—24);
> Group Three (Numbers 25—36).

Give each group five minutes to skim their chapters and to jot down everything God provided or did to sustain Israel while in the wilderness. Come back together as a whole group and make a list on a chalkboard, flipchart or overhead of all that God provided in the wilderness.

Say, **No matter what we decide to take into the wilderness, it will not be enough to sustain us over a long period of time. The only thing that will last and sustain us in the wilderness is God's provision. In Numbers, we discover that everything that Israel needed God provided. Now find a partner, and the two of you use the next few minutes to thank God in prayer for all that He provides to you and your family on your life's journey.**

SECTION THREE: GOD'S SON (10 MINUTES)

JESUS CHRIST REVEALED IN LEVITICUS AND NUMBERS

Objective: To understand how Jesus Christ is portrayed as the Sacrifice for sin in Leviticus and our "Lifted-Up One" in Numbers.

Divide into two groups. Assign one of the following Scripture lists to each group and write the sentence that needs to be completed for each group. Give the groups five minutes to complete their sentences.

Scripture List One: Leviticus 16:1-22; Hebrews 9; 1 John 2:2

Complete this sentence: Jesus Christ as our High Priest is now

(What's discovered should include making intercession for us; forgiving us through His shed blood; giving us confidence and boldness to approach God's throne in prayer.)

Scripture List Two: Numbers 21:6-9; John 3:14,15; 1 Peter 2:23-25

Complete this sentence: When Jesus Christ is lifted up, He

_____.

(Part of the answer would be that He heals, delivers, saves and redeems us defeating the works of Satan and the curse of sin and death.)

With the whole group, discuss:

In what ways do we as God's people experience Jesus as High Priest in our daily walk with Him?

When we lift Jesus up in worship and in our daily lives, what will happen?

PURSUING GOD (5 MINUTES)

NEXT STEPS I NEED TO TAKE

Objective: To make a realistic assessment of one's relationship with Jesus and how that relationship might grow closer in the coming week.

Have each person find the partner they had earlier. Ask them to complete these sentences:

The way I need to serve Him is _____.

What I learned about the wilderness that I need to practice in my daily walk with God is _____.

PRAYER (5 MINUTES)

SEEKING GOD'S GUIDANCE IN PRAYER

Objective: To close this session in worship and prayer to break the bondage of fear.

Read Matthew 4:10 to the group and say, **In this session we have learned from Leviticus and Numbers ways the Israelites worshiped the Lord God.**

Have the whole group form a prayer circle and invite those who wish to complete this sentence:

I worship the Lord God because

_____.

Now invite those who are facing giants in their lives and are fearful, to stand in the middle of the group and ask the other group members to place their hands on their shoulders as you pray this prayer for them: **Almighty God, just as You defeated Israel's enemies, provided their every need and saved them, we ask that You would defeat these "giants" and break every bondage of fear in each person here, in Jesus' mighty name. Amen.**

Session 5 Bible *Tuck-In*™

UNDERSTANDING LEVITICUS AND NUMBERS

The purpose of this session is:
- To provide an overview of the books of Leviticus and Numbers;
- To discover how Jesus Christ is portrayed in Leviticus as our Sacrifice for sin and in Numbers as our "Lifted-Up One."

KEY VERSES

"I am the Lord who brought you up out of Egypt to be your God; therefore be holy, because I am holy." Leviticus 11:45

"The cloud of the Lord was over them by day when they set out from the camp. Whenever the ark set out, Moses said, 'Rise up, O Lord! May your enemies be scattered; may your foes flee before you.' Whenever it came to rest, he said, 'Return, O Lord, to the countless thousands of Israel.'" Numbers 10:34-36

"Now the people complained about their hardships in the hearing of the Lord, and when he heard them his anger was aroused." Numbers 11:1

---

25. Complete this sentence: When Jesus Christ is lifted up, He

_____.

With the whole group, discuss:
In what ways do we as God's people experience Jesus as High priest in our daily walk with Him?
When we lift Jesus up in worship and in our daily lives, what will happen?

PURSUING GOD (5 MINUTES)

NEXT STEPS I NEED TO TAKE
- Have each person find the partner they had earlier. Ask them to complete these sentences:
The way I need to serve Him is _____
What I learned about the wilderness that I need to practice in my daily walk with God is _____

PRAYER (5 MINUTES)

SEEKING GOD'S GUIDANCE IN PRAYER
- Read Matthew 4:10 to the group and say, In this session we have learned from Leviticus and Numbers ways the Israelites worshiped the Lord God.
- Have the whole group form a prayer circle and invite those who wish to complete the following sentence:
I worship the Lord God because _____
- Now invite those who are facing giants in their lives and are fearful, to stand in the middle of the group and ask the other group members to place their hands on their shoulders as you pray this prayer for them: Almighty God, just as You defeated Israel's enemies, provided their every need and saved them, we ask that You would defeat these "giants" and break every bondage of fear in each person here, in Jesus' mighty name. Amen.

SECTION ONE: GOD'S STORY (20 MINUTES)

LEVITICUS AND NUMBERS: LEARNING TO WORSHIP GOD AND COUNTING THE TRIBES

- Tell the group the Bible story doing the suggested activities as you come to them. Distribute the handouts so group members can take notes and refer to them at the appropriate times.

OPTION ONE: (FOR A 90-MINUTE SESSION) The Burnt Offering (15 Minutes)

- Make a list of everything the group suggests. Then as a group, choose the three most difficult things to surrender.

- Divide the group into pairs. Invite them to share with their partners what the most difficult thing to surrender as a burnt offering to the Lord is or has been in their lives (see Romans 12:1,2). Have them pray for each other. Then gather the group back together.

- Say, **Our burnt offering is to sacrifice all we are and have to the Lord.**

SECTION TWO: GOD'S PERSON (20 MINUTES)

JOSHUA AND CALEB: WILLING TO TRUST GOD AND POSSESS THE LAND

- Briefly summarize the story of the 12 spies found in Numbers 13. Put on a chalkboard, flipchart or overhead these two headings:

    Joshua and Caleb   The Other Spies

- Suggest and list the attitudes and qualities Joshua and Caleb had and the attitudes and qualities the other spies had.

- Invite those who wish to share with the whole group about a time in their lives when they faced "giants in the land." Request

---
Fold
---

that some share missed opportunities and how they wandered in a wilderness and experienced God's discipline. Give an example from your own life. Request that others share how God helped them defeat a giant in their lives. Take time to hear three or four testimonies in these areas.

OPTION TWO: (FOR A 90-MINUTE SESSION) The Wilderness Experience (15 minutes)

- Give every group five minutes to decide on a list of things to take into the wilderness. Bring everyone back together and share their lists. As the leader, make a master list of all the items.

- With the whole group, eliminate anything that will perish soon after the journey begins. Ask, **What three things does the group believe they need which would be essential for survival?**

- Now assign each of the three groups a set of 12 chapters from Numbers: Group One: Numbers 1—12, Group Two: Numbers 13—24; Group Three: Numbers 25—36

- Give each group five minutes to skim their chapters and to jot down everything God provided or did to sustain Israel.

SECTION THREE: GOD'S SON (10 MINUTES)

JESUS CHRIST REVEALED IN LEVITICUS AND NUMBERS

- Divide the group into two groups. Assign the following Scriptures to each group and write the sentence that needs to be completed for each group. Give the groups five minutes to complete their sentences.

    Scripture List One: Leviticus 16:1-22, Hebrews 9; 1 John 2:2. Complete this sentence: Jesus Christ as our High Priest is now

---

Scripture List Two: Numbers 21:6-9; John 3:14,15; 1 Peter 2:23-

AN OVERVIEW OF LEVITICUS AND NUMBERS

1. God revealed a pattern of worship to Israel.

   Notes:

2. God who is holy and pure demands a people who are holy and pure (see Leviticus 1—5).

   Notes:

The Burnt Offering pictures the _____ of Jesus for the world.
The Meal Offering pictures the _____ of Christ in life.
The Peace Offering pictures the _____ of Christ in life.
The Sin Offering pictures the _____ of Christ for sin.
The Trespass Offering pictures the _____ by Christ for the demands of God.

3. The priests of the tribe of Levi presented to God the sacrifices, prayers and praises of God's people (see Leviticus 6—10; Numbers 3).

   Notes:

4. The five sacrificial offerings spoke of the blood that atoned for sin and the eight feasts spoke of the food that sustained. Both are of God (see Leviticus 11—27; Numbers 15; 18—19).

   Notes:

CONTINUED

5. As Israel left Mount Sinai, God provided for their needs and prepared them to enter the Promised Land of Canaan (see Numbers 10—12).

Notes:

6. After sending twelve spies into Canaan, Israel learned there were giants in the land. Only Caleb and Joshua urged going forward and possessing the land (see Numbers 13).

Notes:

7. Moses disobeyed God, striking a rock in anger to get water for the people. Both Israel and Moses failed God's test of faithfully obeying and trusting His leading. (see Numbers 14—36)

Notes:

Before next week's session, read:
Sunday: Forward March (Deuteronomy 1:6-46)
Monday: Instructions (Deuteronomy 5:1-33; 6:4-18)
Tuesday: The Messiah, Prophet (Deuteronomy 18:15-22)
Wednesday: God's Covenant (Deuteronomy 30:1-20)
Thursday: The Song of Moses (Deuteronomy 32:1-44)
Friday: God's Blessing (Deuteronomy 33:1-29)
Saturday: The Death of Moses (Deuteronomy 34:1-12)

CONTENT OR COMPLAINING?

Read Philippians 4:4-9; 19 and Numbers 11:1-3.

1. When facing difficulties, I usually am:

_____

Content   Complaining

2. When I experience lack, I usually rely on:

_____

God's resources   Other's resources   My resources

3. When things don't go my way, I usually:

_____

Worry   Despair   Wait on God

4. When enemies attack, I:

_____

Get even   Get angry   Get depressed   Lean on God

5. When problems don't get resolved, I am:

_____

Patient   Impatient

6. When I face problems, I:

_____

Blame God   Blame myself   Blame others   Seek God

7. My attitude toward trials and suffering is:

_____

All joy   Depression

In what way are you least like Israel in the wilderness?

_____

In what way are you most like Israel in the wilderness?

_____

How can your partner pray for you?

_____

Understanding Deuteronomy

The purpose of this session is:

* To provide an overview of the book of Deuteronomy;
* To discover how Jesus Christ is portrayed in Deuteronomy as our True Prophet.

In this session, group members will learn:

* Key truths about God's story in the book of Deuteronomy;
* That Jesus Christ is revealed in Deuteronomy;
* The basic principle of obedience—following God's law with one's mind, will, feelings and actions;
* How to apply basic truths in Deuteronomy to their own lives.

KEY VERSES

"Hear, O Israel: The LORD our God, the LORD is one. Love the LORD your God with all your heart and with all your soul and with all your strength. These commandments that I give you today are to be upon your hearts. Impress them on your children. Talk about them when you sit at home and when you walk along the road, when you lie down and when you get up. Tie them as symbols on your hands and bind them on your foreheads. Write them on the doorframes of your houses and on your gates." Deuteronomy 6:4-9

"And now, O Israel, what does the LORD your God ask of you but to fear the LORD your God, to walk in all his ways, to love him, to serve the LORD your God with all your heart and with all your soul, and to observe the LORD's commands and decrees that I am giving you today for your own good?" Deuteronomy 10:12,13

"See, I set before you today life and prosperity, death and destruction. For I command you today to love the LORD your God, to walk in his ways, and to keep his commands, decrees and laws; then you will live and increase, and the LORD your God will bless you in the land you are entering to possess." Deuteronomy 30:15,16

BEFORE THE SESSION

* Pray for group members by name asking the Holy Spirit to teach them the spiritual truths in Deuteronomy.

- Read chapter 6 in *What the Bible Is All About*.
- Prepare copies of Session 6 handout "An Overview of Deuteronomy" for every group member.
- Check off these supplies once you have secured them:
  ____ Write the following chart on a chalkboard, flipchart or overhead before the session. Mix up the order in each column so that the pairs will have to arrange them correctly.

Bible Book	Event	Jesus Christ's Portrayal
Genesis Creator	Creation and the Beginnings of Nations and Israel	Jesus Christ portrayed as our God
Exodus	God's People Leave Egypt and Receive God's Law	Jesus Christ portrayed as our Passover Lamb
Leviticus	Worship God	Jesus Christ portrayed as our Sacrifice for sin
Numbers	Israel's Wilderness Wanderings	Jesus Christ portrayed as our "Lifted Up One"
Deuteronomy	The Law Repeated	Jesus Christ portrayed as our True Prophet

  ____ Newsprint or posterboard and felt-tip pens if you chose to do Option One.
  ____ Extra Bibles, pencils and paper for group members.
- If you are having a 90-minute session, then carefully read the two option sections right now and pull together any supplies you need for them.
- Read the entire session and look up every passage. Have your Bible *Tuck-In*™ ready for yourself.
- Memorize the key verses: Deuteronomy 6:4,5. Be familiar with the other key verses. Share them periodically in the session and ask the group to repeat them after you.

SECTION ONE: GOD'S STORY (20 MINUTES)

DEUTERONOMY: THE LAW REPEATED

Objective: To tell God's story in Deuteronomy so that the group members will understand how God desired a covenant relationship with Israel and clearly instructed them concerning the blessings of obedience and the curses of disobedience.

Read aloud the following, doing the suggested activities as you come to them. Distribute the handout "An Overview of Deuteronomy" so group members can take notes.

Once again, God spoke through Moses giving His law to Israel before the people entered the Promised Land.

The book of Deuteronomy, meaning "the second law or the repetition of the law," is a collection of Moses' final orations to the people of Israel before his death and their entrance into Canaan. Deuteronomy is the last book in the Pentateuch—the five books of Moses.

Genesis tells of creation, the beginnings of nations and the beginning of God's chosen people, Israel.

Exodus relates the organization of the people into a nation and the giving of the law.

Leviticus tells the way this people were to worship God.

Numbers gives the story of the wanderings of this people.

Deuteronomy relates the final preparation for entering the Promised Land.

Deuteronomy covers only about a two months span of time, including the thirty days of mourning for Moses.

As people arrive, have them form groups of five or six each. With the lists of "Bible Books," "Events" and "Jesus Christ's Portrayals" on a chalkboard, flipchart or overhead, instruct the groups to arrange the lists in the right order. Once every group has completed this, go over the correct order with the whole group.

Moses' first address *Looked Back* from God's perspective at Israel's wanderings in the wilderness (see Deuteronomy 1—9).

Israel was reminded of how spies had been sent out to Canaan and had returned with the report of a land flowing with milk and honey. However, the people rebelled against God, and did not enter the land due to their fear of the giants there. So for forty years, God had them wander in the wilderness until the deaths of all those over 20 years of age who had rebelled. Only Caleb and Joshua were left alive of those adults who had come out of Egypt. Again, they stood on the threshold of destiny. The Promised Land lay before them and now they prepared to possess it.

As a class, explore together what Israel should have learned about God and themselves up to this point. On a chalkboard, flipchart or overhead write the title, "Lessons in the Wilderness." With the whole group, make a list of all the lessons that Israel should have learned from the time they left Egypt until they reached the Promised Land. That list might include these lessons:

• God delivers from slavery and bondage.

- God is mightier than any pagan god or idol.
- God's presence is revealed in a cloud of fire and glory.
- God's law is life.
- God can provide for every need—clothing, food, health, water, etc.
- God defeats the enemies of Israel.
- God punishes and disciplines those who rebel against Him.
- God desires holiness and purity.
- God blesses His people.
- God uses people to prophesy His Word.
- God is a miracle-working God.
- God keeps His promises.
- God leads His people through the wilderness.
- God has provided for redemption through the shedding of blood.
- God desires worship and praise.
- God answers prayer.
- God protects His people.
- God desires total surrender and dependence on Him.
- God heals.

Share a specific lesson you are currently learning then invite volunteers to share which lesson they are learning and to share how God is working in their lives through that lesson.

Moses' second address *Looked Up*, emphasizing Israel's relationship with God and obedience to God's commandments (see Deuteronomy 10—26).

In Deuteronomy 12:1, we read what God says: "These are the decrees and laws you must be careful to follow in the land that the Lord, the God of your fathers, has given you to possess—as long as you live in the land."

Lead the group in reading and repeating Deuteronomy 10:12,13. Divide the class into five sections and assign each section to read in unison one of the five actions God asks: fear, walk, love, serve and observe. After reading the verse aloud several times, invite comments on why each action is important.

Moses' final address *Looked Out* into the future describing the blessings Israel would receive for obeying God and the curses that would result from disobedience (see Deuteronomy 26—33).

Deuteronomy 27 and 28 describe the blessings God promised Israel if they obeyed Him and the terrible curses that would come on Israel for disobedience— they would be scattered, restless and sorrowful. Israel has experienced the truth of these words through the centuries. These warnings are followed by a renewal

of the covenant between God and His people, with promises of blessing and prosperity if they "obey the LORD your God and keep his commands and decrees" (Deuteronomy 30:10). Moses called the people to choose God's way, the way of life (see Deuteronomy 30:11-20). Joshua, at 80 years of age, was commissioned to lead Israel into the Promised Land (see Deuteronomy 31). Moses, at 120 years old, sang a prophetic song of blessing to Israel (see Deuteronomy 32, 33). Finally, he went to a place overlooking the Promised Land (see Deuteronomy 34). There Moses died and God buried him. After 30 days of mourning his death, the people were ready to possess the land under Joshua's leadership.

Ask everyone to form groups of three or four. Ask each small group to look at the list of blessings in Deuteronomy 28:1-14. Have one person read this section of Scripture while each person identifies from the list one blessing he or she has experienced in the last few months and a blessing each one is seeking from the Lord. Some of those blessings include:

- The land prospers;
- The family prospers;
- An abundance of food and life's necessities;
- The defeat of enemies;
- Financial prosperity.

After everyone has shared, have them pray for one another in their small groups.

OPTION ONE: (FOR A 90-MINUTE SESSION)

The Shema (15 Minutes)

Before class, put up on the walls in each of the four corners of the room a piece of newsprint or posterboard. On each sheet , have one of these titles:

    Heart   Soul   Strength   Neighbor as Self

Say to the group, **Deuteronomy 6:4-9 is the Jewish confession called the** *Shema,* **meaning "hear." This confession is recited daily by pious Jews and is recited during worship in the synagogue. Jesus lifted up this commandment including the word "mind" and added to it Leviticus 19:28, "Love your neighbor as yourself," declaring that these were the two greatest commandments (see Matthew 22:37-39). By heart, the Hebrew meant one's mind, thoughts and feelings. Soul referred to the breath of life, the inner self of a person. Strength refers to one's physical being and actions.**

This commandment demands a faithful love for and obedience to the Lord with our total beings. Around the room I have placed pieces of paper (or poster-board) with a label on each. In a moment, you will be placed in a group at one of these pieces of paper. As a group, take a felt-tip pen and have everyone write one way we love God in that area of our lives.

Divide the group into four groups and send each group to one of the four corners of the room where they will have three minutes to write on that particular theme. Every three minutes call time and have the groups move in a clockwise direction to the next title.

After all the groups have made the complete rotation, with the whole group discuss:

What kinds of things get in the way of keeping these commandments?

What consequences did Israel suffer when she failed to keep these commandments? (Enemies defeated her, crops failed, injustice filled the land, the poor suffered, idol worship increased, etc.)

What consequences do we suffer when we fail to keep these commands?

SECTION TWO: GOD'S PERSON (20 MINUTES)

MOSES: TEACHER OF GOD'S LAW

Objective: To understand and follow Moses' example as a teacher of God's Word to our children, families and the people of God.

Say, **The Old Testament depicts men and women as real people with strengths and weaknesses. Moses had wonderful strengths and serious weaknesses. What were his character traits and what can we learn from Moses? He was a great teacher of God's law to Israel as she had to build a foundation in the wilderness as a nation and society. Moses taught Israel God's law so she could worship, receive forgiveness, handle social problems, establish a legal system, fight her enemies, and so forth. On your handout is a list of Scriptures lifting up some of Moses' qualities. With a partner, read your Scriptures and discover the kind of person, teacher and prophet of God Moses was.**

Have the whole group divide into groups of four and work on the handout together. Assign some groups to start from the top of the list, others to start from the bottom and others in the middle. Let them spend about 10-12 minutes together and then bring the whole group back together. Discuss the following:

What qualities did Moses have that are important for Christian leaders to have today?

What lessons of leadership did Moses learn that we can implement in the church today?

OPTION TWO: (FOR A 90-MINUTE SESSION)

God's Covenant (15 Minutes)

Have the whole group divide into four smaller groups and assign each small group four segments of the Law to discuss. Ask them to look up the following passages for each area and to discuss the questions you have written on a chalkboard, flipchart or overhead:

> Group One: False Accusation (see Deuteronomy 19:15-21);
> Group Two: Inheritance (see Deuteronomy 21:15-17);
> Group Three: Fruit of Labor (see Deuteronomy 26:1-15);
> Group Four: Social Order (see Deuteronomy 16:18-20; 22:1-5).

Put the following questions for discussion up on a chalkboard, flipchart or overhead for each group to discuss:

As a group, decide on one law from the Old Covenant that remains a valid practice for our society.

As a group, decide which area of the law would benefit our society most if people were to observe it faithfully?

How could the church maintain the spirit of God's law without becoming legalistic? How valid are these laws for Christians to follow? Why?

Gather the whole group and share the main points each small group concluded in their discussions.

SECTION THREE: GOD'S SON (10 MINUTES)

JESUS CHRIST REVEALED IN DEUTERONOMY

Objective: To discover how Jesus Christ is portrayed as our True Prophet in Deuteronomy.

Say, Remember that God commands His people in Leviticus 11: 44,45 to be holy as He is holy (cf. 1 Peter 1:16 and Matthew 5:48). **Our problem is that there is no way we can be holy in and of ourselves. We need help in being purified and washed clean by a blood sacrifice. God tells Israel in Deuteronomy 18 that the nations around Israel will involve themselves with all sorts of false prophets, sorcery, witchcraft and the occult, but Israel is not permitted to listen to these. Rather, she must hear and obey a true prophet in her midst that God will raise up. "The Lord your God will raise up for you a prophet like me from among your own brothers. You must listen to him"** (Deuteronomy 18:15). **God continues to tell the people how to recognize a true prophet** (see vv. 18-22).

Jesus came to Israel centuries later speaking God's Word to Israel but she refused to listen. Jesus said that prophets were without honor in their own country (see Matthew 13:57). **The main criteria for knowing if a prophet was a true prophet was if his words came true.**

As a group, try to recall some of the major prophetic sayings of Jesus that came true. (This list may include times when He spoke healing and it happened; the times He spoke of His death and resurrection and they happened; the destruction of Jerusalem and the Temple; the betrayal of Judas, Peter's denials, etc.) Read to the group John 5:36-40.

Discuss the following as a group:

Since Jesus' prophetic words about Himself were true, why didn't those religious leaders who knew the law of Moses so well not believe in Jesus?

If someone gives a prophetic word today, how will we know if it's true?

What prompts people to follow false prophets like fortune readers and psychics?

What kinds of false prophets must we avoid (see Deuteronomy 18:9-13)?

PURSUING GOD (5 MINUTES)

NEXT STEPS I NEED TO TAKE

Objective: To have each person reflect on his or her obedience to God's law and call.

Ask each person to spend time in silent reflection and prayer over these questions:

1. **Am I loving the Lord my God with all my heart, soul, mind and strength and my neighbor as myself?**
2. **Am I avoiding all forms of evil, witchcraft, the occult and sorcery?**
3. **What blessings from the Lord am I seeing in my life?**
4. **Are there any curses in my life that need to be broken and purged by the blood of Christ?**
5. **Am I possessing the land—fulfilling the call—that God has placed in my life?**

PRAYER (5 MINUTES)

SEEKING GOD'S GUIDANCE IN PRAYER

Objective: To close the session in prayer seeking God's guidance in obeying His law.

Ask three or four people to share a testimony of how God has blessed their lives or broken a curse in their lives.

After these people have shared, ask everyone to share the completion of this sentence: **God has blessed me to be a blessing by** _____.

As the group leader, close the session in prayer after everyone has shared.

Session 6 Bible *Tuck-In*™

UNDERSTANDING DEUTERONOMY

The purpose of this session is:

- To provide an overview of the book of Deuteronomy;
- To discover how Jesus Christ is portrayed in Deuteronomy as our True Prophet.

KEY VERSES

"Hear, O Israel: The LORD our God, the LORD is one. Love the LORD your God with all your heart and with all your soul and with all your strength. These commandments that I give you today are to be upon your hearts. Impress them on your children. Talk about them when you sit at home and when you walk along the road, when you lie down and when you get up. Tie them as symbols on your hands and bind them on your foreheads. Write them on the doorframes of your houses and on your gates." Deuteronomy 6:4-9

"And now, O Israel, what does the LORD your God ask of you but to fear the LORD your God, to walk in all his ways, to love him, to serve the LORD your God with all your heart and with all your soul, and to observe the LORD's commands and decrees that I am giving you today for your own good?" Deuteronomy 10:12,13

"See, I set before you today life and prosperity, death and

----- Fold -----

If someone gives a prophetic word today, how will we know if it's true?

What prompts people to follow false prophets like fortune readers and psychics?

What kinds of false prophets must we avoid (see Deuteronomy 18:9-13)?

PURSUING GOD (5 MINUTES)

NEXT STEPS I NEED TO TAKE

- Ask each person to spend time in silent reflection and prayer over the following questions:

1. Am I loving the Lord my God with all my heart, soul, mind and strength and my neighbor as myself?

2. Am I avoiding all forms of evil, witchcraft, the occult and sorcery?

3. What blessings am I seeing from the Lord in my life?

4. Are there any curses in my life that need to be broken and purged by the blood of Christ?

5. Am I possessing the land—fulfilling the call—that God has placed in my life?

PRAYER (5 MINUTES)

SEEKING GOD'S GUIDANCE IN PRAYER

- Ask three or four people to share a testimony of how God has blessed their lives or broken a curse in their lives.

- After these people have shared, ask everyone to share the completion of this sentence: "God has blessed me to be a blessing by

  _____."

- As the group leader, close the session in prayer after everyone has shared.

destruction. For I command you today to love the LORD your God, to walk in his ways, and to keep his commands, decrees and laws; then you will live and increase, and the LORD your God will bless you in the land you are entering to possess." Deuteronomy 30:15,16

SECTION ONE: GOD'S STORY (20 MINUTES)

DEUTERONOMY: THE LAW REPEATED

- Tell the group the Bible story doing the suggested activities as you come to them. Distribute the handout "An Overview of Deuteronomy" so group members can take notes.

OPTION ONE: (FOR A 90-MINUTE SESSION)

The Shema (15 Minutes)

- Put up on the walls in the four corners of the room a piece of newsprint (or posterboard). On each piece of newsprint (or posterboard), have one of these titles: "Heart," "Soul," "Strength," "Love Neighbor as Self."
- Tell the group about Deuteronomy 6:4–9.
- Divide the group into four groups and send each group to one of the four corners of the room where they will have three minutes to write on that particular theme.
- After all the groups have made the complete rotation, with the whole group discuss:

SECTION TWO: GOD'S PERSON (20 MINUTES)
MOSES: TEACHER OF GOD'S LAW

- Tell the group about Moses as God's teacher.
- Have the whole group divide into groups of four and work on the handout together. Let the groups spend about 10-12 minutes together and then bring the whole group back together and discuss:

- Fold -

What qualities did Moses have that are important for Christian leaders to have today?
What lessons of leadership did Moses learn that we can implement in the church today?

OPTION TWO: (FOR A 90-MINUTE SESSION)

God's Covenant (15 Minutes)

- Have the whole group divide into four small groups and assign each small group four segments of the Law to discuss.

> Group 1: False Accusation (see Deuteronomy 19:15-21)
> Group 2: Inheritance (see Deuteronomy 21:15-17)
> Group 3: Fruit of Labor (see Deuteronomy 26:1-15)
> Group 4: Social Order (see Deuteronomy 16:18-20; 22:1-5)

- Put the listed questions for discussion up on a chalkboard, flipchart or overhead for each group to discuss.
- Gather the whole group and share the main points each small group concluded in their discussions.

SECTION THREE: GOD'S SON (10 MINUTES)

JESUS CHRIST REVEALED IN DEUTERONOMY

- Tell the group about the True Prophet in Deuteronomy 18.
- As a group, try to recall some of the major prophetic sayings of Jesus that came true. (This list may include times when He spoke healing and it happened; the times He spoke of His death and resurrection and they happened; the destruction of Jerusalem and the Temple and that happened; the betrayal of Judas, Peter's denials, etc.) Read to the group John 5:31-47.
- Discuss:

Since Jesus' prophetic words about Himself were true, why didn't those religious leaders who knew the law of Moses so well not believe in Jesus?

An Overview of Deuteronomy

1. Once again, God spoke through Moses giving His law to Israel before the people entered the Promised Land.

   Notes:

2. Moses' first address *Looked Back* from God's perspective at Israel's wanderings in the wilderness (see Deuteronomy 1—9).

   Notes:

3. Moses' second address *Looked Up* emphasizing Israel's relationship with God and obedience to God's commandments (see Deuteronomy 10—26).

   Notes:

4. Moses' final address *Looked Out* into the future describing the blessings Israel would receive for obeying God and the curses that would result from disobedience (see Deuteronomy 26—27).

   Notes:

CONTINUED

MOSES: TEACHER OF THE LAW

Below are listed some Scriptures that reveal the character and leadership qualities of Moses. Share looking up these passages with your group members (about four passages each). Jot down all the qualities and character traits—both good and bad—that Moses exhibited in his life.

Exodus 2:11-17 _____

Exodus 6:1-12 _____

Exodus 14:10-14 _____

Exodus 24:12-18 _____

Exodus 34:29-33 _____

Numbers 12:1-15 _____

Numbers 20:1-12 _____

Deuteronomy 3:21-29 _____

Deuteronomy 31:1-8: _____

Which quality in Moses' life would you like to see grow in your own life?

Before next week's session, read:

Sunday: Joshua's commission (Joshua 1—2)

Monday: Crossing the Jordan (Joshua 3)

Tuesday: The Fall of Jericho (Joshua 6)

Wednesday: The Sin of Achan (Joshua 7)

Thursday: Occupation of the Land (Joshua 11)

Friday: Caleb's Possession (Joshua 14)

Saturday: Joshua's Farewell (Joshua 24)

Understanding Joshua

The purpose of this session is:
- To provide an overview of the book of Joshua;
- To discover how the Bible portrays Jesus Christ in Joshua.

In this session, group members will learn:
- Key truths about God's story in Joshua;
- That the book of Joshua portrays Jesus Christ as Captain of our salvation;
- The basic principle of biblical success and prosperity—possessing and claiming what God has set before us;
- How to apply basic truths in Joshua to their lives.

KEY VERSES

"Do not let this Book of the Law depart from your mouth; meditate on it day and night, so that you may be careful to do everything written in it. Then you will be prosperous and successful. Have I not commanded you? Be strong and courageous. Do not be terrified; do not be discouraged, for the LORD your God will be with you wherever you go." Joshua 1:8,9

"Now fear the LORD and serve him with all faithfulness. Throw away the gods your forefathers worshiped beyond the River and in Egypt, and serve the LORD. But if serving the LORD seems undesirable to you, then choose for yourselves this day whom you will serve, whether the gods your forefathers served beyond the River, or the gods of the Amorites, in whose land you are living. But as for me and my household, we will serve the LORD." Joshua 24:14,15

BEFORE THE SESSION

- Pray for group members by name asking the Holy Spirit to teach them the spiritual truths in Joshua.
- Read chapter 7 in *What the Bible Is All About*.
- Prepare copies of the Session 7 handouts "An Overview of Joshua" and "Joshua—A Godly Leader" for every group member.
- Check off these supplies once you have secured them:
  ____ Copies of the handout for each group member
  ____ Index cards.
  ____ Extra Bibles, pencils and paper for the group.

_____ If you are doing Options 1 and 2, write the list on a chalkboard, flipchart or overhead.

- If you are having a 90-minute session, carefully read the two option sections right now and pull together any supplies you need for them

- Read the entire session and look up every passage. Have your Bible _Tuck-In_™ ready for yourself.

- Arrive early and be ready to warmly greet each group member as he or she arrives.

- Memorize the key verses. Share them periodically in the session and ask the group to repeat them after you.

SECTION ONE: GOD'S STORY (20 MINUTES)

JOSHUA: GOD SAVES

Objective: To provide an overview of how the book of Joshua tells God's story of giving victory, success and prosperity to Israel in possessing the land of Canaan.

Read aloud the following, doing the suggested activities as you come to them. Distribute the handout "An Overview of Joshua" so group members can take notes.

Anticipation dominated Deuteronomy. Possession dominates Joshua.

As people arrive, have them look in Joshua 1 for promises and instructions God made to His people. As they find one have them write it on a chalkboard or posterboard.

Before Entering the Promised Land

<u>Promises</u>   <u>Instructions</u>

Through Moses, God led Israel through the Red Sea out of bondage in Egypt, provided them with a vision of faith, gave them the law and ways to worship Him, and brought them to the brink of the Promised Land. Through Joshua, God led Israel through the Jordan River into Canaan to live a life of faith and to possess the Promised Land. The book of Joshua has two great parts: The Conquest of the Promised Land in chapters 1—12 and The Occupation of the Promised Land in chapters 13—24.

PART ONE—CONQUERING THE LAND (SEE JOSHUA 1—13)

Mobilize the people! Forward march (see Joshua 1—4)!

In the wilderness, Israel walked by sight led by the cloud and pillar of fire of God's presence. Israel lived by God's provision of manna, water, meat and clothing. In Canaan, Israel had to walk and live by faith. The cloud and provisions were no longer visible. After renewing the covenant given to them, reciting the blessings of obedience and the curses of disobedience, crossing Jordan and setting up a memorial to the Lord, Israel is now armed and dangerous. Prepared and tested by the wilderness, Israel mobilizes to face her first battle in the Promised Land—Jericho.

With the whole group, list on a chalkboard, flipchart or overhead all the things that Israel could remember God doing for them during the Exodus in the wilderness. (For example, setting them free from slavery; defeating their enemies; providing for their needs; keeping them healthy, fed and clothed; giving them the Law and the ways to worship God; anointing elders to minister to them; etc.)

Think about ways that we set up memorials as believers to remember what God has done. As a group, list some of those memorials (The Lord's Supper, baptism, reading the Word, teaching and discipling others, building houses of worship, giving, serving, etc.).

Victory at Jericho, but defeat at Ai—Sin in the camp (see Joshua 4—9).

Two critical lessons are learned immediately at the start by Israel. First, battles are planned and won God's way not man's. Second, sin is never a private matter. The sin of one person infects the whole people. Israel does not storm Jericho by her own might and strength. God brings the walls down His way and in His timing. When one man, Achan, disobeys God, the nation suffers defeat at Ai. Achan's private sin becomes a corporate matter. In Adam, humanity fell. In Achan, the nation suffered defeat.

Corporate personality is a key concept for understanding Scripture. The blessings or curses upon one affect the whole just as the blessings and curses upon the whole touch each individual. In God's economy, then one man, Jesus—perfect and sinless—can die for all humanity and His victory over sin and death can be participated in by all who trust Him (see Romans 5:12-21).

Divide the whole group into two. One group will look at Rahab in Joshua 2:1-7,15,16, 22-24 and the other will look at Achan in Joshua 7:1-12,20-26. Have each group determine the actions Rahab or Achan took and the effects of their actions on Israel. After five minutes have them discuss their findings.

The southern and northern campaigns partially conquers the land (see Joshua 10—11).

As Israel conquers the land, two important lessons must be noted: First, God fought for Israel and gave her victory. "All these kings and their lands [in the south] Joshua conquered in one campaign, because the LORD, the God of Israel, fought for Israel" (Joshua 10:42). "So Joshua took the entire land [after the northern campaign], just as the LORD had directed Moses, and he gave it as an inheritance to Israel according to their tribal divisions. Then the land had rest from war" (Joshua 11:23). Second, the whole land was *not* conquered. The peoples not driven out as God had commanded would introduce idol worship and war against Israel in the future.

In groups of four, have each person in the group choose one of the following Scripture verses and then share who the Israelites did *not* conquer. The Scriptures are:

Joshua 13:2-5,13   Joshua 15:63 and 16:10   Joshua 17:12,13   Joshua 21:43-45

Have the groups circle on the map the areas left unconquered and then discuss the following:

Since all the Canaanites were not destroyed, what problems might that cause Israel in the future?

When we allow enemies and sin to continue to exist in our lives, what happens to us?

PART TWO—POSSESSING AND DIVIDING THE LAND (JOSHUA 13—24)

The land was possessed and divided according to God's will (see Joshua 13—14).

The strong did not take the best part of the land because they were strong, leaving the fragments for the weak. Neither did the rich purchase the choicest spots leaving the poor the more undesirable spots. The land was allotted according to God's plan. Though all of the land was allotted to the various tribes, it was not all conquered until the time of David. All that was subdued at this time was the mountainous land; the cities and the plains were hardly touched.

Caleb chose a hard inheritance (see Joshua 14).

Remember that of the original 12 spies who scouted out the land only Joshua and Caleb wanted to take the land. Caleb's attitude was unchanged. Though the walled cities would be hard to take, Caleb asked Joshua that those would be his inheritance, saying "The LORD helping me, I will drive them out just as he said" (Joshua 14:12). At the age of 85, Caleb didn't cower from God's command to be strong and courageous. He trusted God for the victory.

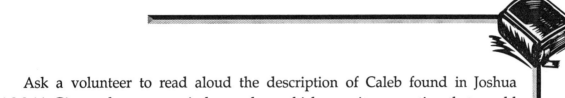

Ask a volunteer to read aloud the description of Caleb found in Joshua 14:8,9,14. Give each person an index card on which to write one action that would be evidence of his or her desire to follow God wholeheartedly. Do not have them write their names on the card. Collect the cards and pass them out again randomly. Have volunteers read aloud the cards they receive.

Joshua's farewell is a challenge to obey and serve the Lord (see Joshua 24).

"But as for me and my household, we will serve the Lord" (Joshua 24:15). These words were echoed by the Israelites. However, after Joshua's death many turned to the pagan gods of the Canaanites. With God comes blessing. Separated from Him, Israel encountered curse and tragedy.

Option One (For a 90-Minute Session)

God's Battle Plan (15 Minutes)

Say to the group: **Let's list the steps of God's battle plan for taking Jericho.** With the group, discuss and agree upon the plan while you list the steps on a chalkboard, flipchart or overhead. Your list might include:

1. Carrying the ark, the priests march around the city in front of the people with an armed guard in front and back.
2. Seven priests blow trumpets while marching in front of the people.
3. The marching once around the city continued for six days with the people remaining quiet.
4. On the seventh day, the ark, priests, army and people marched around the city seven times and on the seventh time the people shouted.

Discuss the following:

• **When did God deliver Jericho into the hands of the Israelites?** (See Joshua 6:2).

• **What was the point of the marching and trumpets?**

• **Why do you suppose that God used Rahab, the prostitute? What importance did she have in Israel's future?** (See Matthew 1:5; Hebrews 11:31; and James 2:25).

• **It's interesting to note that when Hebrews 11 lists the heroes of faith, Joshua is never mentioned by name though Rahab and the battle of Jericho are mentioned. What does this suggest to you?** (It took more faith to trust God from inside the city than outside.)

- When a battle or victory is won in your life, in what ways can you give glory to God?

SECTION TWO: GOD'S PERSON (20 MINUTES)

JOSHUA: SOLDIER FOR THE LORD

Objective: To understand how to be strong and courageous in the Lord and becoming prosperous and successful through His strength and Word.

Joshua didn't become a leader overnight. God prepared him for leadership. Joshua also learned valuable lessons as a soldier for God during the conquest of Canaan. Being a soldier for the Lord requires faithfulness to the commanding officer. "No one serving as a soldier gets involved in civilian affairs—he wants to please his commanding officer" (see 2 Timothy 2:4). What did Joshua do that pleased the Lord? How did God prepare Joshua? What qualities of a godly leader do we see in Joshua that we can imitate in our own lives?

Have everyone fill in the section of their Session 7 handouts entitled "Joshua—A Godly Leader." Divide everyone into groups of four. Instruct each person in each group to select one or two qualities and look up the Scripture. Then have them share in their small groups those qualities they discovered and evaluate themselves based on those qualities. Finally ask each person to share his or her strongest qualities and the one quality that needs the most growth.

OPTION TWO (FOR A 90-MINUTE SESSION)

Facing Your Jericho (15 Minutes)

A significant battle plan is revealed by God in Joshua 1—6. There are some battle principles revealed in these chapters. Write the following principles on a chalkboard, flipchart or overhead and invite group members to jot them down on a piece of paper.

Fighting Battles God's Way

1. Be strong and courageous in the Lord.
2. Be willing to commit to total victory.
3. Do not give the enemy a foothold.
4. Declare that the battle belongs to the Lord.
5. Praise Him for the victory before the battle begins.
6. Fight the battle His way not yours.
7. Keep God's word ever in your heart and mouth.
8. Don't take any personal glory for the victory.
9. Give God all glory and praise for every victory.
10. Don't go into battle unprepared.

In pairs, share which principles you find to be the hardest to apply in your personal life and why. Then share a time when God won a great battle in your life and give Him the glory and praise for that to the other group members.

SECTION THREE: GOD'S SON (10 MINUTES)

JESUS CHRIST REVEALED IN JOSHUA

Objective: To explore how Jesus Christ is revealed as Captain of our salvation.

Before the battle of Jericho, Joshua meets the commander of the Lord's army. This is known as a theophany—the appearance of the Lord in human form in the Old Testament. Joshua is commanded to remove his shoes for he stands on holy ground. The name Joshua is the Hebrew name for Jesus, which is Greek. Joshua means "God saves."

Have members return to the groups of four and have each person look up one of the following passages and read it to the small group: Genesis 28:17; Exodus 3:5; Acts 7:33; Revelation 19:11-14.

Discuss the following questions:

- **When we come into the Lord's presence, what should our response be?**
- **In what ways is Jesus Christ the Captain of our salvation?** (He defeated the works of Satan; defeated sin and death; destroyed the power of evil; gave us abundant and eternal life)
- **How is Joshua, an earthly commander, like Jesus Christ our heavenly Captain?** (He does only what the Father commands; he waits on God to save; he gives all glory to God; he recognizes that the battle belongs to the Lord.)

PURSUING GOD (5 MINUTES)

NEXT STEPS I NEED TO TAKE

Objective: To take a realistic assessment of one's relationship with Jesus and how that relationship might grow closer in the coming week.

Look again at the qualities of godly leadership which Joshua exhibited. Which of these qualities do you need God's Spirit to cultivate in your life? Find a partner and share with that partner the qualities that need to grow in your life. Pray for one another.

PRAYER (5 MINUTES)

SEEKING GOD'S GUIDANCE IN PRAYER

Objective: To close the session with affirmation and intercession in pairs.

Say to the pairs, **Share with a partner a recent battle you have faced or are facing. Tell your partner what you have been doing to try to win the battle. Share what you need to let go of in order for the battle to belong to the Lord. As your partner prays silently for you, pray out loud:**

Lord, I surrender _____ in my life so that You and You alone can be Captain of my life and my battles. Amen.

Bring the whole group together and turn to Joshua 24:14-24 which is called the "Covenant Renewal Ceremony." As the leader, you read Joshua's part and have the class read Israel's part as a closing affirmation to the Lord.

Session 7 Bible *Tuck-In*™

UNDERSTANDING JOSHUA

The purpose of this session is:

- To provide an overview of the book of Joshua;
- To see Jesus Christ revealed as the Captain of our salvation in the book of Joshua.

KEY VERSES

"Do not let this Book of the Law depart from your mouth; meditate on it day and night, so that you may be careful to do everything written in it. Then you will be prosperous and successful. Have I not commanded you? Be strong and courageous. Do not be terrified; do not be discouraged, for the LORD your God will be with you wherever you go." Joshua 1:8,9

"Now fear the LORD and serve him with all faithfulness. Throw away the gods your forefathers worshiped beyond the River and in Egypt, and serve the LORD. But if serving the LORD seems undesirable to you, then choose for yourselves this day whom you will serve, whether the gods your forefathers served beyond the River, or the gods of the Amorites, in whose land you are living. But as for me and my household, we will serve the LORD." Joshua 24:14,15

---

exhibited. Which of these qualities do you need God's Spirit to cultivate in your life?

- Find a partner and share with that partner the qualities that need to grow in your life. Pray for one another.

PRAYER (5 MINUTES)

SEEKING GOD'S GUIDANCE IN PRAYER

- Say to the pairs: Share with a partner the most recent battle you have faced or are facing. Tell your partner what you have been doing to try to win the battle. Share what you need to let go of in order for the battle to belong to the Lord. As your partner prays silently for you, pray out loud:

  Lord, I surrender _____ in my life so that You and You alone can be Captain of my life and my battles. Amen.

- Bring the whole group together and turn to Joshua 24:14-24 which is called the "Covenant Renewal Ceremony." As the leader, you read Joshua's part and have the class read Israel's part as a closing affirmation to the Lord.

SECTION ONE: GOD'S STORY (20 MINUTES)

JOSHUA: GOD SAVES

- Tell the group the Bible story doing the suggested activities as you come to them. Distribute the handout "Overview of Joshua' so group members can take notes.

OPTION ONE (FOR A 90-MINUTE SESSION)

God's Battle Plan (15 Minutes)

- With the group discuss the steps to God's battle plan and list the following on a chalkboard, flipchart or overhead.

- Discuss the following:
  When did God deliver Jericho into the hands of the Israelites? (See Joshua 6:2).
  What did the army do to capture the city?
  Why do you suppose that God used Rahab, the prostitute?
  What importance did she have in Israel's future? (See Matthew 1:5; Hebrews 11:31; and James 2:25).
  It's interesting to note that when Hebrews 11 lists the heroes of faith, Joshua is never mentioned by name though Rahab and the battle of Jericho is mentioned. What does this suggest to you? (That Joshua is a humble servant; that God gets the glory for victory not Joshua.)
  When a battle or victory is won in your life, in what ways can you give glory to God?

SECTION TWO: GOD'S PERSON (20 MINUTES)

JOSHUA: SOLDIER FOR THE LORD

- Describe how Joshua became a godly leader.

- Have everyone fill out the section of the Session 7 handouts entitled "Joshua—A Godly Leader."

- Divide everyone into groups of four. Instruct each person in the small groups to choose one or two qualities and look up the Scriptures. Then have everyone share what they discovered about their chosen qualities with their small groups and evaluate themselves based on those qualities.

- Finally ask each person to share his or her strongest qualities and the one quality that needs the most growth.

OPTION TWO (FOR A 90-MINUTE SESSION)

Facing Your Jericho (15 Minutes)

- Have the battle principles written on a chalkboard, flipchart or overhead.

- A significant battle plan is revealed by God in Joshua 1—6. Here are some battle principles revealed in these chapters.

- In pairs, share which principles you find to be the hardest to apply in your personal life and why. Then share a time when God won a great battle in your life and give Him the glory and praise for that to the other group members.

SECTION THREE: GOD'S SON (10 MINUTES)

JESUS CHRIST REVEALED IN JOSHUA

- In small groups, ask the group members to share at least three ways they can see Jesus revealed in Joshua.

PURSUING GOD (5 MINUTES)

NEXT STEPS I NEED TO TAKE

- Look again at the qualities of godly leadership which Joshua

An Overview of Joshua

Anticipation Dominated Deuteronomy. Possession Dominates Joshua.

Notes:

Part One—Conquering the Land

1. Mobilizing the people. Forward march! (Joshua 1—4).

Notes:

2. Victory at Jericho, but defeat at Ai! Sin in the camp (Joshua 4—9).

Notes:

3. The southern and northern campaigns—possessing the land (Joshua 10—11).

Notes:

CONTINUED

PART TWO—POSSESSING AND DIVIDING THE LAND (JOSHUA 13—24)

1. The land was possessed and divided according to God's will.

Notes:

2. Caleb chose a hard inheritance (Joshua 14).

Notes:

3. Joshua's farewell is a challenge to obey and serve the Lord (Joshua 24).

Notes:

Before next week's session, read:

Monday: Priests (Exodus 29, 39; Leviticus 13, 16; Joshua 21; 1 Samuel 2:12-36; 2 Chronicles 7)

Tuesday: Judges (Judges 1—2; 1 Samuel 9, 16)

Wednesday: Kings (1 Samuel 8, 9, 16; 1 Kings 1—2; 2 Kings 17:1-8; 23)

Thursday: Prophets (1 Kings 18—2 Kings 8; 2 Kings 19—20; 2 Chronicles 15; Isaiah 6; Jeremiah 1)

Friday: Jesus as Priest and Prophet (Hebrews 4:14-16; Matthew 13:57; John 4:19)

Saturday: Jesus as Judge and King (John 5:30; 2 Timothy 4:1; Matthew 25:40; Revelation 17:14)

JOSHUA—A GODLY LEADER

Read each passage and then identify the quality of godly leadership that Joshua exhibited or learned. Then put an X on the line based on how strong that quality is in your life right now.

Scripture	Quality	Self-Evaluation	
Exodus 17:9-15	_____	Strong _____	Weak
Exodus 24;12,13	_____	Strong _____	Weak
Exodus 33:11	_____	Strong _____	Weak
Numbers 11:27-29	_____	Strong _____	Weak
Numbers 14:1-10,30,38	_____	Strong _____	Weak
Numbers 27:18-23	_____	Strong _____	Weak
Deuteronomy 1:35-38	_____	Strong _____	Weak
Deuteronomy 31:7,8	_____	Strong _____	Weak
Deuteronomy 34:9	_____	Strong _____	Weak
Joshua 1:1-3	_____	Strong _____	Weak
Joshua 3:5-7	_____	Strong _____	Weak
Joshua 4:8-11	_____	Strong _____	Weak
Joshua 5:3-9	_____	Strong _____	Weak
Joshua 5:13-15	_____	Strong _____	Weak
Joshua 6:25	_____	Strong _____	Weak
Joshua 7:1-13	_____	Strong _____	Weak
Joshua 9:1-12	_____	Strong _____	Weak
Joshua 24:15	_____	Strong _____	Weak

Understanding the Period from Judges Through Esther

The purpose of this session is:

* To provide an overview of Judges through Esther;
* To see Jesus Christ portrayed in the leadership offices of Israel—priest, judge, king and prophet.

In this session, group members will learn:

* Key truths about God's story in the period spanning the judges through the return of the captives to Jerusalem;
* That the whole of Scripture portrays Jesus Christ as the coming Messiah;
* That Israel continually strayed and broke covenant with God;
* How to apply basic truths in Scripture to their own lives.

KEY VERSES

"And the LORD said to Moses: 'You are going to rest with your fathers, and these people will soon prostitute themselves to the foreign gods of the land they are entering. They will forsake me and break the covenant I made with them. On that day I will become angry with them and forsake them; I will hide my face from them, and they will be destroyed. Many disasters and difficulties will come upon them, and on that day they will ask, "Have not these disasters come upon us because our God is not with us?"'" Deuteronomy 31:16,17

BEFORE THE SESSION

* Pray for group members by name asking the Holy Spirit to teach them the spiritual truths in Judges through Esther.
* Read chapter 13 and skim chapters 8-12 and 14 in *What the Bible Is All About*.
* Prepare copies of Session 8 handout, "Overview of God's Story," for every group member.

- Have copies of Session 8 handout, "When Events Happened" strips for every 3-5 people in the group. After you have copied these handouts for the group members, cut each handout along the dotted lines and mix up the order so that the group members can put them back into chronological order. Paper clip the set of strips together.
- Check off these supplies once you have secured them:
  - ____ Make all the copies that you need for this session.
  - ____ Have a rope with at least four woven strands.
  - ____ Have a sharp knife or blade that can cut thick rope.
  - ____ Have a permanent ink felt-tip pen.
- If you are having a 90-minute session, then carefully read the two option sections right now and pull together any supplies you need for them.
- Read the entire session and look up every passage. Have your Bible *Tuck-In*™ ready for yourself.
- Arrive early and be ready to warmly greet each group member as he or she arrives.
- Memorize the key verses. Share them periodically in the session and ask the group to repeat them after you.

SECTION ONE: GOD'S STORY (20 MINUTES)

ISRAEL: GOD'S LOVE FOR AN ADULTEROUS PEOPLE

Objective: To discover how the cycle of repentance and apostasy continued through the time of Israel settling the Promised Land, the monarchy, the divided kingdom and the exile.

As people arrive, pass out the "When Events Happened" strips and ask people to work in groups of no more than five people to put them in order. Review the correct order with the group and then give everyone a copy of Session 8 handout, "When Events Happened."

Read aloud the following, doing the suggested activities as you come to them. Distribute the handout "Overview of God's Story from Judges to Esther" so group members can take notes.

Assign half of the groups to match the people and their actions, while the other half matches the portraits of Jesus Christ with the books. Then have them share their results with the whole group.

Give the following instructions to those working on the people and their actions: **On your handout, "An Overview of God's Story from Judges to Esther,"** there is a matching exercise to review the people that God used to communicate His covenant and purposes to humanity. Match the people with their actions.

Give the following instructions to those working on the portraits of Jesus Christ: **Complete the portraits of Jesus Christ from each book as you recall them. I'll give you the answers in a moment.**

(The following are the correct answers to the matching and completion exercises on the handout.):

Adam and Eve	Desired to be as gods
Noah	Only man in his time that God found righteous
Abraham, Isaac and Jacob	Patriarchs who trusted God
Joseph	Saved his family from famine bringing them to Egypt
Moses	Obeyed God to lead Israel out of Egypt
Joshua	A commander who fought God's battles
Rahab	A traitor who helped God's people

Genesis portrays Jesus Christ as our Creator God.
Exodus portrays Jesus Christ as our Passover Lamb.
Leviticus portrays Jesus Christ as our Sacrifice for sin.
Numbers portrays Jesus Christ as our "Lifted-Up One."
Deuteronomy portrays Jesus Christ as our True Prophet.
Joshua portrays Jesus Christ as Captain of our salvation.

Have people remain in the same small groups. Assign each group the first three peaks of Bible history. Ask them to list the important points they can remember about the assigned peaks. Give them about four minutes to do this, then share their lists with the whole group. Affirm the groups' efforts and then summarize:

At Peak One, God created a perfect universe and human beings to be in a relationship or covenant with Him. Humanity broke the relationship, separating themselves from God through rebellious sin!

At Peak Two, God began the process of rebuilding a covenant relationship with humanity through the faith and trust of one man—Abraham, the father of God's people called the Hebrews, who became the nation of Israel. Enslaved in Egypt, God called Moses to lead His people out of Egypt into freedom.

At Peak Three, on Mount Sinai God gave His law and the order of worship to Israel. After refusing to enter the Promised Land, Israel wandered 40 years in the wilderness, learning to depend on and obey God. With only Joshua and Caleb left alive from those who had left Egypt, God used Joshua to lead Israel across the Jordan and conquer Canaan.

The Old Testament is the shadow of the substance to come in Jesus Christ. As Hebrews 10:1 says, "The law is only a shadow of the good things that are coming—not the realities themselves." Each book points to the coming Messiah—the second Adam—Who will redeem humanity from sin and death through the sacrifice of His own blood. The whole law and order of worship given to Israel portrays the relationship, life and sacrifice of Jesus, who lived the highest life, the perfect covenant relationship with the Father and with us.

We left Israel in Canaan, adjusting from a life as nomads to one of agriculture and city dwelling. In the wilderness, they walked by sight following God's visible presence in the form of a cloud or a pillar of fire and depending totally on His provisions. In Canaan, Israel needed to walk by faith. However, they turned to their neighbors—the Canaanites still left in the land—to learn farming, city life, social customs and most tragic of all, worship. Intended to be God's bride, Israel instead played the harlot and began to worship idols and practice forbidden customs instead of following God's Law.

Read aloud Deuteronomy 31:16,17.

Take the woven rope and knife. Ask for two volunteers. Have them take the rope in their hands and pull it with enough tension to make it straight, leaving about a foot between them. Tape a sign with the word, "Covenant" on that section of rope. Now cut a major strand of the rope and say, **Some Israelites in the North began following the idolatrous ways of the surrounding peoples.** (Cut another strand of the rope.) **Then the Israelites began to intermarry and adapt to the religions and lifestyles of surrounding peoples, rather than living lives holy and separate unto the Lord. The judges could only rescue them for a season** (see Judges 1—1 Samuel 7). **Israel asked for a king** (see 1 Samuel 8). **God gave Israel a king—Saul. He disobeyed God** (see 1 Samuel 13—15). **Then David, a man after God's own heart, was anointed king to replace Saul** (see 1 Samuel 16). **He finally destroyed the Philistines and united the nation. When David died, his son Solomon became king. Wise at first, Solomon built the Temple** (see 1 Kings 5:5). **But after marrying hundreds of foreign wives, Solomon not only allowed temples to be built for worshiping idols** (see 1 Kings 11); **he even ended up worshiping idols himself. After Solomon's death, the nation split into two kingdoms—the Northern Kingdom of Israel and the Southern Kingdom of Judah.** (Cut another strand in the rope.)

The prophets of God, like Elijah, Amos and Isaiah, called God's people back to Him. However, the Northern Kingdom of Israel continued to worship idols under wicked kings, the most notorious of whom was Ahab who married Queen Jezebel. Finally in 732 B.C., Israel was destroyed and carried into exile by Assyria, never to return again to the Promised Land. (Cut the final strands until only a few threads are left in the rope.) **While the Southern Kingdom of Judah still had the Temple and some righteous kings like Uzziah, Hezekiah and Josiah, idol worship was still allowed which caused widespread injustice and unrighteousness. After**

becoming a vassal state of Babylon, Jerusalem and the Temple were finally destroyed in 580 B.C. and Judah was carried off into exile. (Cut the rope down to only one thread.) During the exile the Jewish people were saved from extinction through the heroic actions of Mordecai and Queen Esther. After some 40 years in exile, Nehemiah and Ezra were permitted to return to rebuild Jerusalem and the Temple, and to reinstitute the worship of God. God's covenant with Israel and for that matter, with humanity, hung by a thread. The remnant of the Jewish people was the only solitary link with the past, with the patriarchs—Abraham...Isaac...Jacob...Moses...Joshua...the Judges...King David...and the prophets of God.

That link, that remnant of the covenant relationship was enough for God to use to bring history to its climax. At just the right time, in the fullness of time (see Galatians 4:4), the Messiah—the Savior—the Christ would come.

Now that we have previewed what is to come, let's explore some of the main themes of the upcoming studies.

OPTION ONE: (FOR A 90-MINUTE SESSION)

Three Kings (15 Minutes)

Divide the group into four smaller groups. Make these assignments:

> Group One: 1 Samuel 8:1—15:35 (Saul)
> Group Two: 1 Samuel 16—27, 2 Samuel (David)
> Group Three: 1 Kings 1—11 (Solomon)
> Group Four: 2 Kings 18—20; 2 Chronicles 29—32 (Hezekiah)

Instruct each group to take seven minutes to skim the chapters and section titles in their Bibles for their particular king. Have them jot down some of the big events in that king's reign. After seven minutes, bring all the groups back to share what they have found. As they report, list some of their major findings on a chalkboard, flipchart or overhead under each king's name. Then discuss with the whole group:

What happened in the relationship between each king and the Lord?

How did each king's relationship with God affect the nation of Israel?

Why was David called a man after God's own heart?

SECTION TWO: GOD'S PEOPLE (20 MINUTES)

OF PRIESTS, JUDGES, KINGS AND PROPHETS

Objective: To understand how Israel's leaders both maintained and also broke the covenant with God from the judges through the exile.

Divide the whole group into four smaller groups. Give each group the assignment to research information about each of the kinds of leaders that Israel had in her history—priests, judges, kings and prophets. Ask that each small group have one person who will report back to the whole group a summary of their findings.

After about ten minutes of researching these texts and filling in their handouts, bring the whole group back together and ask the reporters of each small group to brief the whole group. As the small groups report, make a list on a chalkboard, flipchart or overhead of the main points made by each group. That list might look something like this:

Priests	Judges	Kings	Prophets
Anointed and consecrated	Led the people in military actions against her enemies	Anointed to be king	Chosen by God
Ministered in the Tabernacle and Temple	Gave some political leadership	Military and political leaders of Israel	Persecuted
High priest went to God for answers	Given God's Spirit to lead	Their sins affected the whole nation	Spoke God's truth
At times, disobeyed God	Resolved disputes	After David, many led Israel away from God	At times, did did miracles
			Foresaw the coming Messiah

Priests: Exodus 29; 39; Leviticus 13; 16; Joshua 21; 1 Samuel 2:12-36; 2 Chronicles 7

Judges: Skim the book of Judges and 1 Samuel 9; 16.

Kings: 1 Samuel 8; 9; 16; 1 Kings 1—2, 2 Kings 17:1-8; 23

Prophets: Skim 1 Kings 18—2 Kings 8; 2 Kings 19—20; Chronicles 15; Isaiah 6; Jeremiah 1.

    With the whole group discuss:

Why did Israel have a problem following God once she settled in the Promised Land?

How did the judges and kings help Israel follow God?

How did they lead her astray?

Why were the prophets in every age so persecuted?

OPTION TWO: (FOR A 90-MINUTE SESSION)

Two Kingdoms (15 Minutes)

Assign half of the group to complete Assignment One and the other half to complete Assignment Two.

       Assignment One: 2 Chronicles 10—36. (Focus your survey on the Southern Kingdom, Judah.)

       Assignment Two: 1 Kings 12—2 Kings 17. (Focus your survey on the Northern Kingdom, Israel.)

    Say, **Within each group, divide up the chapters so that each person has an equal number of chapters to survey. Simply skim through the chapters to see the direction each kingdom was taking in their relationship to God and how the citizens and kings acted toward God and one another. Jot down a few notes to answer the following questions:** (Write these on a chalkboard, flipchart or overhead.)

Which kings led the people toward God?

Which ones away from God?

How did the prophets try to lead people back to God?

Was the covenant relationship improving or breaking apart in this period?

    Gather the whole group together after about ten minutes and have a general discussion of the above questions. The general consensus will be in the direction that both kingdoms were headed away from God, the Northern Kingdom more rapidly than the Southern. While there were some godly kings in the south (none in the north), both would eventually end up being exiled. God's prophets sought to bring the people and kings back to repentance and obeying the Law. At times in the south, the people and kings would repent for a season, but then they would return to injustice and unrighteousness.

SECTION THREE: GOD'S SON (10 MINUTES)

JESUS CHRIST REVEALED IN THE OFFICES OF PRIEST, JUDGE, KING AND PROPHET

Objective: To see how each office of leadership in the Old Testament was a fore-shadowing of the coming Messiah who would save us.

Remember that the whole of the Old Testament foreshadows and points to the coming Messiah, the Anointed One of Israel. Each office of leadership in Israel is fulfilled in our one true Leader—Jesus Christ.

Have the group members look up these passages with you and ask one person to read each passage out loud when you come to it. Discuss the questions following each passage:

Read Hebrews 4:14-16. How does Jesus Christ function as our High Priest? What authority and power does He have that earthly priests do not have?

Read John 5:30; 2 Timothy 4:1. How will Jesus Christ function as a Judge? How is that different from the judges of Israel? How is it similar?

Read Matthew 25:40; Luke 23:3; John 1:49; Revelation 17:14. How is Jesus Christ a fulfillment of the kingly line of David? Over what kingdom does Jesus rule?

Read Matthew 5:10; Acts 2:22,23; 7:51,52. How was Jesus Christ persecuted like the prophets of old?

PURSUING GOD (5 MINUTES)

NEXT STEPS I NEED TO TAKE

Objective: To take a realistic assessment of one's relationship with Jesus and how that relationship might grow closer in the coming week.

God's people in the Old Testament continued in a destructive cycle of repen-

tance and then rebellion, of seeking God and then forsaking Him, of obedience and then wickedness. What do you have in your spiritual walk that can safeguard you from this destructive cycle? Here is a list of some of the ways we maintain our spiritual lives:

Write the list on a chalkboard, flipchart or overhead for the group members to see:

Prayer	Bible study	Being in an accountability group
Worship regularly	Sharing my faith	Memorizing God's Word
Giving to God	Serving God	Avoiding temptation

Other: (List any others that come to your mind.)

After reading the list, share your answers to the following questions with your partner.

Which one helps you the most to stay fixed on Jesus Christ?

Which one needs more cultivation in your life?

Have everyone get into pairs and share with their partners how they might stay fixed on Jesus.

PRAYER (5 MINUTES)

SEEKING GOD'S GUIDANCE IN PRAYER

Objective: To close this session with affirmation and intercession in pairs.

Ask each pair to share their completions of the following with one another:

One spiritual lesson I learned today was _____.

One way I need to be disciplined in obeying God is _____.

Have the pairs pray for God's Spirit to guide them in all truth and empower one another to walk in His ways.

Session 8 Bible *Tuck-In*™

UNDERSTANDING JUDGES THROUGH ESTHER

The purpose of this session is:

- To provide an overview of the Bible from Judges through Esther;
- To see Jesus Christ portrayed in the leadership offices of Israel—priest, judge, king and prophet.

KEY VERSES

"And the LORD said to Moses: 'You are going to rest with your fathers, and these people will soon prostitute themselves to the foreign gods of the land they are entering. They will forsake me and break the covenant I made with them. On that day I will become angry with them and forsake them; I will hide my face from them, and they will be destroyed. Many disasters and difficulties will come upon them, and on that day they will ask, "Have not these disasters come upon us because our God is not with us?"'" Deuteronomy 31:16,17

SECTION ONE: GOD'S STORY (20 MINUTES)

ISRAEL: GOD'S LOVE FOR AN ADULTEROUS PEOPLE

- Tell the group the Bible story doing the suggested activities as you

---

PURSUING GOD (5 MINUTES)

NEXT STEPS I NEED TO TAKE

- Divide the group into pairs and have them share ways they can avoid the kind of destructive cycle Israel got into when she repented and then rebelled against God.
- Write the list on a chalkboard, flipchart or overhead for the group members to see:

Prayer	Bible study
Worship regularly	Sharing my faith
Memorizing God's Word	Serving God
Being in an accountability	Giving to God
group	Avoiding temptation

Other: (List any others that come to your mind.)

- After reading the list, share your answers to the following questions with your partner.

Which one helps you the most to stay fixed on Jesus Christ?

Which one needs more cultivation in your life?

PRAYER (5 MINUTES)

SEEKING GOD'S GUIDANCE IN PRAYER

- Ask the partners in each pair to share their completions of the following with one another:

One spiritual lesson I learned today was _____.

One way I need to be disciplined in obeying God is _____.

- Have the pairs pray for God's Spirit to guide them in all truth and empower one another to walk in His ways.

come to them. Distribute the handout "An Overview of God's Story of Judges through Esther" so group members can take notes.

OPTION ONE: (FOR A 90-MINUTE SESSION)

THREE KINGS (15 MINUTES)

- Divide the group into four smaller groups. Make these assignments:

  Group One: 1 Samuel 8:1—15:35 (Saul)
  Group Two: 1 Samuel 16—27, 2 Samuel (David)
  Group Three: 1 Kings 1—11 (Solomon)
  Group Four: 2 Kings 18—20; 2 Chronicles 29—32 (Hezekiah)

- Instruct each group to take seven minutes to skim the chapter and section titles in their Bibles for their particular king. Have them jot down some of the big events in that king's reign. After seven minutes, bring all the groups back to share what they have found. As they report, list some of their major findings. Then discuss with the whole group the listed questions.

SECTION TWO: GOD'S PERSON (20 MINUTES)

Of Priests, Judges, Kings and Prophets

- Divide the whole group into four smaller groups. Give each group the assignment to research information about each of the kinds of leaders that Israel had in her history—priests, judges, kings and prophets. Ask them to prepare a summary of their findings.

- After about ten minutes of researching these texts and filling in their handouts, ask the reporters of each small group to brief the whole group. As the small groups report, make a list of the main points.

OPTION TWO: (FOR A 90-MINUTE SESSION)

Two Kingdoms (15 Minutes)

- Assign half of the group to complete Assignment One and the

— Fold —

other half to complete Assignment Two.

Assignment One: 2 Chronicles 10—36 (Focus on Judah.)
Assignment Two: 1 Kings 12—2 Kings 17 (Focus on Israel.)

- Within each group, divide up the chapters so that each person has an equal number of chapters to survey. Simply skim through the chapters to see the direction each kingdom was taking in their relationship to God and how the citizens and kings acted toward God and one another.

- Gather the whole group together after about ten minutes and have a general discussion of the above questions.

SECTION THREE: GOD'S SON (10 MINUTES)

JESUS CHRIST REVEALED IN THE OFFICE OF PRIEST, JUDGE, KING AND PROPHET

- Remember that the whole of the Old Testament foreshadows and points to the coming Messiah, the Anointed One of Israel. Each office of leadership in Israel is fulfilled in the one true Leader—Jesus Christ.

- Have the group members look up these passages with you and ask one person to read each passage out loud when you come to it. Discuss the questions following each passage:

  Read Hebrews 4:14-16. How does Jesus Christ function as our High Priest? What authority and power does He have that earthly priests do not have?

  Read John 5:30; 2 Timothy 4:1. How will Jesus Christ function as a Judge? How is that different from the judges of Israel? How is it similar?

  Read Matthew 25:40; Luke 23:3; John 1:49; Revelation 17:14. How is Jesus Christ a fulfillment of the kingly line of David? Over what kingdom does Jesus rule?

  Read Matthew 5:10; Acts 2:22,23; 7:51,52. How was Jesus Christ persecuted like the prophets of old?

AN OVERVIEW OF GOD'S STORY
OF JUDGES THROUGH ESTHER

Matching God's people and their actions: (Draw a line from the person(s) to the correct action.)

Adam and Eve	Obeyed God to lead Israel out of Egypt
Noah	Patriarchs who trusted God
Abraham, Isaac and Jacob	A traitor who helped God's people
Joseph	A commander who fought God's battles
Moses	Only man in his time that God found righteous
Joshua	Desired to be as gods
Rahab	Saved his family from famine bringing them to Egypt

Complete each portrait of Jesus Christ:

Genesis portrays Jesus Christ as _____.

Exodus portrays Jesus Christ as _____.

Leviticus portrays Jesus Christ as _____.

Numbers portrays Jesus Christ as _____.

Deuteronomy portrays Jesus Christ as _____.

Joshua portrays Jesus Christ as _____.

1. At Peak One, God created a perfect universe and human beings to be in a relationship or covenant with Him.

   Notes:

2. At Peak Two, God began the process of rebuilding a covenant relationship with humanity through the faith and trust of one man—Abraham, the father of God's people called the Hebrews, who became the nation of Israel.

   Notes:

CONTINUED

3. At Peak Three, on Mount Sinai God gave His law and order of worship to Israel.

   Notes:

4. The Old Testament is the shadow of the substance to come in Jesus Christ. As Hebrews 10:1 says, "The law is only a shadow of the good things that are coming—not the realities themselves."

   Notes:

5. We have left Israel in Canaan, adjusting from a life as nomads to one of agriculture and city dwelling.

   Notes:

6. That link, that remnant of covenant relationship was enough for God to use to bring history to its climax. At just the right time, in the fullness of time (see Galatians 4:4), the Messiah—the Savior—the Christ would come.

OF PRIESTS, JUDGES, KINGS AND PROPHETS

Write a brief description of the characteristics and responsibilities of:

Priests

CONTINUED

Judges

Kings

Prophets

Before next week's session, read:
Sunday: Only Partial Victories (Judges 1—2:5)
Monday: Institution of the Judges (Judges 2:16—3:11)
Tuesday: Deborah and Barak (Judges 4:4—5:31)
Wednesday: Gideon, the Farmer (Judges 6:1-16; 7:16-25)
Thursday: Jephthah's Terrible Vow (Judges 11:12-40)
Friday: Samson, the Strong Man (Judges 15 and 16)
Saturday: The Story of Ruth (Ruth)

WHEN EVENTS HAPPENED

FLOOD   BABEL   ABRAHAM   ISAAC

Cut here

JACOB   JOSEPH

Cut here

MOSES

Cut here

JOSHUA, CALEB   MOSES, JOSHUA

Cut here

RAHAB   ACHAN

Cut here

JOSHUA

Understanding Judges and Ruth

The purpose of this session is:

- To provide an overview of Judges and Ruth;
- To discover how Jesus Christ is portrayed in Judges as our Deliverer-Judge and in Ruth as our Kinsman-Redeemer.

In this session, group members will learn:

- Key truths about God's story in Judges and Ruth;
- That the book of Judges portrays Jesus Christ as our Deliverer-Judge and the book of Ruth as our Kinsman-Redeemer;
- The basic principle of humanity's wickedness and constant need of repentance coupled with God's unending mercy in the face of our lack of obedience;
- How to apply basic truths in Scripture to their own lives.

KEY VERSES

"Therefore the LORD was very angry with Israel and said, 'Because this nation has violated the covenant that I laid down for their forefathers and has not listened to me, I will no longer drive out before them any of the nations Joshua left when he died. I will use them to test Israel and see whether they will keep the way of the LORD and walk in it as their forefathers did.' The LORD had allowed those nations to remain; he did not drive them out at once by giving them into the hands of Joshua." Judges 2:20-23

"In those days Israel had no king; everyone did as he saw fit." Judges 17:6

BEFORE THE SESSION

- Pray for group members by name asking the Holy Spirit to teach them the spiritual truths in Judges and Ruth.
- Read chapter 8 in *What the Bible Is All About*.
- Prepare copies of Session 9 handout, "An Overview of Judges and Ruth" for every group member.

- Check off these supplies once you have secured them:
    - ____ Have extra Bibles, pencils and paper for group members.
    - ____ Prepare a shoe box labeled with "Time Capsule" and today's date.
    - ____ Collect a stack of newspapers and magazines that contain ads that portray our lifestyle and provide a few pairs of scissors.
    - ____ If you are going to do Option One with charades for Samson's stories, then have the 3x5-inch cards of the stories written out before class and hand them to people whom you feel would be good at miming the stories. You may give a set of three to two different persons for the two teams or you may give a set of three to two or three people from each team. See Option One for what to put on the cards.
- If you are having a 90-minute session, carefully read the two option sections right now and pull together any supplies you need for them.
- Read the entire session and look up every passage. Have your Bible *Tuck-In*™ ready for yourself.
- Arrive early and be ready to warmly greet each group member as he or she arrives.
- Memorize the key verses. Share them periodically in the session and ask the group to repeat them after you.

SECTION ONE: GOD'S STORY (20 MINUTES)

Objective: To provide an overview of God's story in Judges and Ruth.

Label a small box with the words "Time Capsule" and today's date. Have a stack of newspapers and magazines. As people arrive, tell them to cut out articles and ads that they feel reflect the quality and kind of life in our society and then place them in the "Time Capsule." After collecting a number of items, pull a few pictures out of the time capsule and ask the group how someone finding their "time capsule" in a few hundred years would evaluate us. Then ask how God would evaluate us.

Read aloud the following, doing the suggested activities as you come to them. Distribute the handout "An Overview of Judges and Ruth" so group members can take notes.

The key for understanding Judges is found in Judges 17:6, "In those days Israel had no king; everyone did as he saw fit" (see Judges 1—2).

A repetitive cycle shaped Israel's history between the death of Joshua and the first king, Saul. "The Israelites did evil in the eyes of the LORD...the anger of the LORD burned against Israel" (Judges 3:7,8). Each time Israel broke covenant with God and worshiped idols, God allowed Israel's enemies to attack, persecute and subjugate her.

Have a discussion with the whole group on how this principle of forsaking God and experiencing the attack of enemies and evil on a culture can be seen in our own culture. List on a chalkboard, flipchart or overhead the ways the group members see moral decline and spiritual idolatry in our society today.

What symptoms of moral and spiritual decay do we have in our culture?

What enemies do we face?

How can the tide be turned back to focusing on God?

Remember how all the enemies of Israel had not been driven from the land under Joshua? God used these remaining Canaanites to teach Israel some valuable lessons.

Ask everyone to find a partner and together fill out their handouts under point two after reading Judges 2:10-23. With the whole group discuss:

Why do you suppose that Israel was unable to resist worshiping idols even when it meant the punishment of God and the burden of being enslaved to her enemies?

Whenever Israel had suffered enough under the bondage of her enemies, her people would cry out to the Lord. God would respond by raising up a judge among His people. The Spirit of the Lord would come upon the judges giving them power to throw off the oppression of the enemies (see Judges 3—16).

Divide into groups of no more than five per group. Assign each group one or two times of oppression in Israel's history under the judges. Ask each group to discover in their section what Israel's sin was, the punishment Israel suffered and how God delivered Israel.

Tell the groups to fill in their parts on the handout. After about five minutes call everyone together and have all the groups share what they discovered. Below is a list of the assignments for each group and the suggested points that they may discover.

- **First Oppression, Judges 3:7-11.** (Sin—Idolatry; Punishment—8 years of oppression; Deliverer and judge—Othniel)
- **Second Oppression, Judges 3:12-31.** (Sin—Immorality and idolatry; Punishment—18 years of oppression; Deliverer and judge—Ehud and Shamgar)
- **Third Oppression, Judges 4:1-11.** (Sin—Departed from God; Punishment—20 years of oppression; Deliverer and judge—Deborah and Barak)

- **Fourth Oppression, Judges 6:1-14.** (Sin—Departed from God; Punishment—7 years under the Midianites; Deliverer and judge—Gideon)
- **Fifth Oppression, Judges 8:33—9:5,22-24,50—10:5.** (Sin—Departed from God; Punishment—Civil war, etc.; Deliverer and judge—Tola and Jair)
- **Sixth Oppression, Judges 10:6—11:1.** (Sin—Idolatry increased; Punishment—18 years of oppression under the Philistines and Ammonites; Deliverer and judge—Jephthah [and successors])
- **Seventh Oppression, Judges 13:1-25.** (Sin—Departed from God; Punishment—40 years of oppression by the Philistines; Deliverer and judge—Samson)

With the death of Samson, the kingdom of Israel was anything but united. One word described Israel's state—confusion (see Judges 17—21).

There was confusion in the spiritual life of the nation (see Judges 17—18). **Second, there was confusion in the moral life of the nation** (see Judges 19). **Finally, there is confusion in the political life of the nation** (see Judges 21).

During the leadership of Moses, Joshua and the judges, Israel was governed by a theocracy. At the center of her life was the worship of the living God, obeying His laws and seeking His presence. In your small group discuss:
In a present-day democracy, how can God's people have a godly influence on our government and culture?

In the book of Ruth, we see how God's plan for a king in Israel and for the Messiah progressed as a foreigner named Ruth married Boaz. They became the grandparents of King David from whose line would come the Messiah (see Ruth 1—4).

This story is not merely a heart-warming romance, or an example of how virtue is rewarded. It shows us God's inclusion of all people, not just the chosen Hebrews. Even the despised Moabites have a place in God's plan for humanity.

OPTION ONE: (FOR A 90-MINUTE SESSION)

Samson—Strong and Weak (15 Minutes)

Divide the group into two teams. You will be having some fun with the stories of Samson. Have each team pick three people who will mime a story from Samson's life. The persons miming the story will have one minute for their teams to guess the story. If they cannot guess in one minute, then the other team has fifteen seconds to try to guess the story and "steal" the point. Alternate back and forth between the teams. Make two sets of cards with the following information and hand them out to the mimes.

Team One

Card 1: The Angel of the Lord tells Samson's parents they are going to have a baby though they are barren (see Judges 13).

Card 2: Samson tears a lion apart with his bare hands and later eats honey out of the carcass (see Judges 14).

Card 3: Samson falls in love with Delilah and lies to her about being tied with new ropes. He breaks the ropes easily (see Judges 16).

Team Two

Card 1: The Angel of the Lord tells Samson's parents to dedicate him as a Nazarite meaning he cannot drink wine or cut his hair (see Judges 13).

Card 2: Angry at the Philistines, Samson ties torches to the tails of foxes and lets them run through their crops destroying them with fire (see Judges 15).

Card 3: Blinded by the Philistines, Samson stands between two pillars of their pagan temple built to honor Dagon and pulls down the entire temple, killing everyone (see Judges 16).

After having fun with the charades about Samson, discuss:

What qualities of leadership did Samson have that helped Israel?

What were Samson's weaknesses and how did they affect the whole nation?

SECTION TWO: GOD'S PERSON (20 MINUTES)

GIDEON: A WEAK MAN BECOMES A MIGHTY WARRIOR

Objective: To help group members understand how God uses our weaknesses to manifest His strength and accomplish His will.

Ask the group members to read the story of Gideon with you in Judges 6:11-16; 7:1-22. In the stories about Gideon, two significant spiritual lessons can be seen. Write the following points on a chalkboard, flipchart or overhead:

1. God's delight in using the weak to manifest His strength (see Judges 6:15; Judges 7).

2. The empowering of the Holy Spirit enabling God's servants to do mighty things (see Judges 6:34, note Zechariah 4:6).

Ask the whole group to recall different places in God's story up to this point in the Bible where:

• **God used lowly and humble people to accomplish His purposes.** (The patriarchs and Joseph; Moses; Joshua; Rahab; the judges before Gideon; Ruth.)

• **God's Spirit giving special guidance and power.** (Upon the elders of Israel; giving Moses signs and wonders for Pharaoh; leading Israel out of Egypt; parting the Jordan; overwhelming the walls of Jericho; etc.)

OPTION TWO: (FOR A 90-MINUTE SESSION)

Unlikely Leaders (15 Minutes)

Divide the group into groups of four. Ask each small group to read over the material in Judges 4:1—5:2. Put these sentences on a chalkboard, flipchart or overhead for the groups to see. Ask them to look for the following things as they read:

Leadership qualities that Deborah possessed were

_____.

Leadership qualities that Barak possessed were

_____.

One verse in Deborah's song that particularly inspired me was

_____.

After about ten minutes gather the whole group again. Ask the group to make two lists. One list would be based on their experiences in the world. This list would answer the question, **"What qualities does the world expect in a good leader?"** The second question would be, **"What qualities did God look for in His leaders—especially the judges?"** Put these lists on a chalkboard, flipchart or overhead. Then discuss the following:

How do the lists differ?

How can we identify these qualities in potential leaders for God's people today?

SECTION THREE: GOD'S SON (10 MINUTES)

JESUS CHRIST REVEALED IN JUDGES AS OUR DELIVERER-JUDGE AND IN RUTH AS OUR KINSMAN-REDEEMER

Objective: To understand how these books portray Jesus Christ.

With the whole group participating, complete this sentence in as many ways as possible:

The judges, through God's Spirit and power, rescued Israel from

_____.

Now complete this sentence with the group:

Today, Jesus Christ rescues us from

_____.

Discuss:

In what ways do we need Jesus today as our Deliverer-Judge?

Say to the group: **The story of Ruth is a beautiful love story that portrays the Kinsman-Redeemer love Jesus has for us just as Boaz had for Ruth. Ruth was a Moabitess. These people were descendants of Lot, but they were not Jews; they were Gentiles. In establishing the family which was to produce the world's Savior, God chose a beautiful Gentile girl, led her to Bethlehem and made her the bride of Boaz. This is an example of God's grace. He adopts the Gentiles into Christ's family. Of course we know that, although Ruth was born a Gentile, through her first husband or Naomi, she learned of the true God. Boaz was a descendant of Rahab, the harlot who helped Joshua's spies in Jericho.** (Read Matthew 1:5.) **So we see that David's great-grandmother was a Moabitess and his great-grandfather was part-Canaanite. This is part of the bloodline of the Messiah.**

Ask anyone in the group who did not have Christian parents to share how they came to know Jesus as Savior. Point out to the group that we come into God's grace not because of who our parents are but because of who Jesus is. Invite anyone who wishes to do so to give a prayer of praise for how God's love in Jesus reached out and saved them.

PURSUING GOD (5 MINUTES)

NEXT STEPS I NEED TO TAKE

Objective: To take a realistic assessment of one's relationship with Jesus and how that relationship might grow closer in the coming week.

Write the following lines on a chalkboard, flipchart or overhead. Tell the group that the qualities on the left side of the line are some of the qualities we discovered in the servant-leaders of Judges. Ask the group to form pairs and to share with their partner where they would put themselves on one of the lines right now and also where they would have been five years ago. Share how much growth has occurred and still needs to happen in that quality.

Say, **God uses humble, servant-leaders to accomplish His purposes. Put yourself on the line with the qualities of servant-leaders:**

Humble	**Proud**

Available	**Too busy**

Willing to do things His Way	**Must do things your own way**

PRAYER (5 MINUTES)

SEEKING GOD'S GUIDANCE IN PRAYER

Objective: To close in a group prayer in which group members recognize and confess the need to grow as servant-leaders.

Form a closing circle. Go around the circle with those who wish to do so praying this prayer: **Lord, as a servant-leader I need _____.**

Session 9 Bible *Tuck-In*™

UNDERSTANDING JUDGES AND RUTH

The purpose of this session is:

- To provide an overview of Judges and Ruth;
- To discover how Jesus Christ is portrayed in Judges as our Deliverer-Judge and in Ruth as our Kinsman-Redeemer.

KEY VERSES

"Therefore the LORD was very angry with Israel and said, 'Because this nation has violated the covenant that I laid down for their forefathers and has not listened to me, I will no longer drive out before them any of the nations Joshua left when he died. I will use them to test Israel and see whether they will keep the way of the LORD and walk in it as their forefathers did.' The LORD had allowed those nations to remain; he did not drive them out at once by giving them into the hands of Joshua." Judges 2:20-23

"In those days Israel had no king; everyone did as he saw fit."
Judges 17:6

SECTION ONE: GOD'S STORY (20 MINUTES)

JUDGES AND RUTH

- Tell the group the Bible story doing the suggested activities as

---

share how they came to know Jesus as Savior. Point out to the group that we come into God's grace not because of who our parents are but because of who Jesus is. Invite anyone who wishes to do so to give a praise prayer for how God's love in Jesus reached out and saved them.

PURSUING GOD (5 MINUTES)

NEXT STEPS I NEED TO TAKE

- Write the following lines on a chalkboard, flipchart or overhead.

Tell the group that the qualities on the left side of the line are some of the qualities we discovered about servant-leaders in Judges. Ask the group to form pairs and to share with their partners where they would put themselves on one of the lines right now and also where they would have been five years ago. Share how much growth has occurred and still needs to happen in each quality.

Say, **God uses humble, servant-leaders to accomplish His purposes. Put yourself on the line with the qualities of servant-leaders:**

Humble		Proud

Available		Too busy

Willing to do things His Way	**Must do things your own way**

PRAYER (5 MINUTES)

SEEKING GOD'S GUIDANCE IN PRAYER

- Form a closing circle. Go around the circle with those who wish to do so praying this prayer: **Lord, as a servant-leader I need**

_____

you come to them. Distribute the handout "An Overview of Judges and Ruth" so group members can take notes.

OPTION ONE: (FOR A 90-MINUTE SESSION)

Samson: Strong and Weak (15 Minutes)

- Divide the group into two teams for playing charades based on the life of Samson.

- Give each team one minute to guess. If they cannot guess in one minute, then the other team has fifteen seconds to try to guess the story and "steal" the point. Alternate back and forth between the teams. Discuss the questions.

SECTION TWO: GOD'S PERSON (20 MINUTES)

GIDEON: A WEAK MAN BECOMES A MIGHTY WARRIOR

- Ask the group members to read the story of Gideon with you in Judges 6:11-23; 7:1-22. In the stories about Gideon, two significant spiritual lessons from Judges can be seen:

- Put these points on a chalkboard, flipchart or overhead:

  1. God's delight in using the weak to manifest His strength (see Judges 6:15; Judges 7).

  2. The empowering of the Holy Spirit enabling God's servants to do mighty things (see Judges 6:34, note Zechariah 4:6).

- Ask the whole group to brainstorm about different places in God's Story up to this point in the Bible where:

  God has used lowly and humble people to accomplish His purposes.

  God's Spirit gives special guidance and power.

- With the whole group, make a list of the qualities that God gave Gideon to be a great leader.

-------- Fold --------

OPTION TWO: (FOR A 90-MINUTE SESSION)

Unlikely Leaders (15 Minutes)

- Divide the group into groups of four. Ask each small group to survey and read over the material in Judges 4—5 and to look for the following things: (Write these sentences on a chalkboard, flipchart or overhead.)

  Leadership qualities that Deborah possessed were

  Leadership qualities that Barak possessed were

  One verse in Deborah's song that particularly inspired me was

- After about ten minutes, gather the whole group again. Ask the group to make two lists. One list would be based on their experiences in the world. This list would answer the question, "What qualities does the world expect in a good leader?" The second question would be, "What qualities did God look for in His leaders—especially the judges?

SECTION THREE: GOD'S SON (10 MINUTES)

JESUS CHRIST REVEALED AS DELIVERER-JUDGE AND KINSMAN-REDEEMER

- With the whole group participating, complete this sentence in as many ways as possible:

  The judges through God's Spirit and power rescued Israel from:

- Now complete this sentence with the group:

  Today, Jesus Christ rescues us from _____ .

  Discuss: **In what ways do we need Jesus today as our Deliverer-Judge?**

- Give the background on Ruth to the group.

- Ask anyone in the group who did not have Christian parents to

AN OVERVIEW OF JUDGES AND RUTH

1. The key for understanding Judges is found in Judges 17:6, "In those days Israel had no king; everyone did as he saw fit."

   Notes:

2. Remember how all the enemies of Israel had not been driven from the land under Joshua? God used these remaining Canaanites to teach Israel some valuable lessons (see Judges 1—2).
   Read Judges 2:10-23. Every time you read something that Israel did or did not do in her relationship with God jot it down under, "Sins of Israel." Each time you come across God's response to Israel's sin, jot that down under, "God's Response to Israel's Sins."

   Israel's Sins:

   God's Responses to Israel's sins:

3. Whenever Israel had suffered enough under the bondage of her enemies, her people would cry out to the Lord. God would respond by raising up a judge among His people. The Spirit of the Lord would come upon the judges giving them power to throw off the oppression of the enemies (see Judges 3—16).
   • First Oppression, Judges 3:7-11.
     Sin: _____
     Punishment: _____
     Deliverer and Judge: _____
   • Second Oppression, Judges 3:12-31
     Sin: _____
     Punishment: _____
     Deliverer and Judge: _____

CONTINUED

- Third Oppression, Judges 4:1-11.
  Sin: _____
  Punishment: _____
  Deliverer and Judge: _____

- Fourth Oppression, Judges 6:1-14.
  Sin: _____
  Punishment: _____
  Deliverer and Judge: _____

- Fifth Oppression, Judges 8:33—9:5,22-24,50—10:5.
  Sin: _____
  Punishment: _____
  Deliverer and Judge: _____

- Sixth Oppression, Judges 10:6—11:1.
  Sin: _____
  Punishment: _____
  Deliverer and Judge: _____

- Seventh Oppression, Judges 13:1-25.
  Sin: _____
  Punishment: _____
  Deliverer and Judge: _____

4. With the death of Samson, the kingdom of Israel was anything but united. One word described Israel's state—confusion (see Judges 17—21).

Notes:

CONTINUED

5. In the book of Ruth, we see how God's plan for a king in Israel and for the Messiah progressed, as a foreigner named Ruth married Boaz. They became the great-grandparents of King David from whose line would come the Messiah (see Ruth 1—4).

Boaz as the closest male relative of the widow Ruth, has the responsibility under the law to marry Ruth and provide for children through her since she has none from her first Jewish husband. As such, Boaz is Ruth's kinsman-redeemer. What similarities do you see between this custom and what Christ did for us?

Notes:

Before next week's session, read:
Sunday: Samuel, "Name of God" (1 Samuel 1—3)
Monday: Samuel, the Prophet (1 Samuel 4—7)
Tuesday: Saul, the King (1 Samuel 8—12)
Wednesday: Saul, the Self-Willed (1 Samuel 13—15)
Thursday: David Anointed (1 Samuel 16—18)
Friday: David's Adventures (1 Samuel 19—20; 22; 24)
Saturday: Death of Samuel and Saul (1 Samuel 25—26; 31)

Understanding 1 Samuel

The purpose of this session is:

- To provide an overview of 1 Samuel;
- To discover how Jesus Christ is portrayed as our King in 1 Samuel.

In this session, group members will learn:

- Key truths about God's story in 1 Samuel;
- That Jesus Christ is revealed in 1 Samuel;
- The basic principles of godly leadership—being available, humble, obedient, repentant before God and seeking His way;
- How to apply basic truths in Scripture to their own lives.

KEY VERSES

"But now your [Saul's] kingdom will not endure; the LORD has sought out a man after his own heart and appointed him leader of his people, because you have not kept the LORD's command." 1 Samuel 13:14

"But the Lord said to Samuel, 'Do not consider his appearance or his height, for I have rejected him. The LORD does not look at the things man looks at. Man looks at the outward appearance, but the LORD looks at the heart.'" 1 Samuel 16:7

"All those gathered here will know that it is not by sword or spear that the LORD saves; for the battle is the LORD's, and he will give all of you into our hands." 1 Samuel 17:47

BEFORE THE SESSION

- Pray for group members by name asking the Holy Spirit to teach them the spiritual truths in 1 Samuel.
- Read chapter 9 in *What the Bible Is All About*.
- Prepare copies of Session 10 handouts "An Overview of 1 Samuel" for every group member.

- For Option Two, prepare a large sheet of butcher paper (or a bulletin board or blank area of a wall) with the title "David: A Follower of God; A Leader of Men" written across the top. Draw a line down the middle of the paper. Label the left side "Godliness" and the right side "Leadership." (If you are using a bulletin board or wall, write the titles on paper and attach them with tape.)
- Check off these supplies once you have secured them:
  ____ Prepare an equal number of name tags for three different names—Samuel, Saul and David (enough for each person in your group). The end result will be that you will have three groups, each one named after one of these leaders.
- If you are having a 90-minute session, then carefully read the two option sections right now and pull together any supplies you need for them.
- Read the entire session and look up every passage. Have your Bible *Tuck-In*™ ready for yourself.
- Arrive early and be ready to greet warmly each group member as he or she arrives.
- Memorize the key verses. Share them periodically in the session and ask the group to repeat them after you.

SECTION ONE: GOD'S STORY (20 MINUTES)

Objective: To discover how 1 Samuel tells God's story through three leaders of His people—Samuel, Saul and David.

As people arrive, give each of them a name tag, seeking to distribute an equal number labeled Samuel, Saul and David. Have the class members find everyone else in the class who has the same name that they have. Form three groups—Samuel, David and Saul. Each group is to survey the book of 1 Samuel and collectively answer these questions about the person on their name tags:

What kind of relationship with God did this man have at the beginning of his call into leadership?

When facing stress and temptation, how did this man respond?

To what would you attribute this leader's faithfulness to God or lack of faithfulness?

Ask each group to choose one person who will report back to the whole group. Encourage everyone to take notes about each leader on his or her handout.

Read aloud the following, doing the suggested activities as you come to them. Distribute the handout "An Overview of 1 Samuel" so group members can take notes.

First Samuel is dominated by three of Israel's leaders—Samuel, Saul and David.

Remember our mention of "corporate personality" earlier in Session 7? The whole nation can be represented by one person and one person's destiny is affected by the whole nation. For example, at Jericho the lowliest soldier in Israel's army was a mighty warrior because of the nation's victory through the Lord. And, the defeat of Israel at Ai hinged on the sin of one man—Achan.

God used Samuel, Saul and David to help Israel shape her destiny. Through Samuel, God instituted the monarchy of Israel. Through Saul, God taught the nation the importance of obedience to His ways not man's. Through David, God made an everlasting covenant that out of His seed would come a King and Kingdom that would never end.

Samuel was the last of the judges, the first of the prophets and the founder of the monarchy (see 1 Samuel 1—3).

Notice that the first three chapters of 1 Samuel indicate three important aspects for revival and renewal among God's people. Write these on a chalkboard, flipchart or overhead:

    1. A praying mother (see 1 Samuel 1)
    2. A chastened people (see 1 Samuel 2)
    3. A faithful prophet (see 1 Samuel 3)

Prayer, humility, repentance and a godly spokesman can bring a people back to God. Samuel and Israel began listening to God and recognized they had a need for godly leadership.

With the whole group discuss:

What lessons can we learn from Samuel's leadership of Israel?

After the period of the judges, Israel was in complete cultural, spiritual and political confusion (see 1 Samuel 4—7).

The High Priest Eli was a godly man, but his sons were corrupt and unholy. As a result, the Philistines defeated Israel and captured the ark of God in battle. The Israelite soldiers mistakenly believed that the ark could protect them so they carried it into battle.

Give someone in the group a cross and hand another person a Bible. Ask them **"Will this protect you?"** No matter how they answer, say **"The Bible of God cannot protect you, but the God of the Bible can"** or **"The cross of Christ cannot protect you but the Christ of the cross can."** Do the same thing with a picture of a church or any other religious artifact that you may have. In fact, the whole group should be able to make the reply with you after you do this a few times so invite them to help you shout the reply.

In fact, the ark of God is a very poor substitute for the God of the ark!

Saul is anointed king but then rebels in pride (see 1 Samuel 8—15).

Saul looked great, and started strong, but faithful, spiritual leadership was proven by obedience not appearance.

Assign the following verses to various people in the class. Ask them to read the verse silently and then to determine the sinful attitude or action that Saul committed. Everyone can list these on the handout as they are shared. Remind the group members that they may need to read the whole story around the assigned verse to understand the context of the sinful attitude or action.

If you have more in your group than verses, assign more than one person to each verse.

> 1 Samuel 10:8; 13:7-9 (Saul doesn't follow Samuel's instructions.)
>
> 1 Samuel 13:11,12 (Saul makes excuses instead of repenting.)
>
> 1 Samuel 13:13,14 (Saul disobeyed God.)
>
> 1 Samuel 15:1-9 (Saul disobeyed God.)
>
> 1 Samuel 15:10,11 (Saul turned away from God.)
>
> 1 Samuel 15:12 (Saul pridefully sets up a monument to himself.)
>
> 1 Samuel 15:13-19 (Saul makes excuses and blames others.)
>
> 1 Samuel 15:16-21 (Saul disobeys and does evil in God's eyes.)
>
> 1 Samuel 15:22-24 (Saul has rebelled against God.)
>
> 1 Samuel 15:25,26 (Saul feigns worship—acts religious—but has really rejected the word of God.)
>
> 1 Samuel 15:27-29 (Saul is more concerned with what man [Samuel] thinks than God.)
>
> 1 Samuel 15:30,31 (Saul wants honor or glory that belongs only to God.)

After giving everyone about three minutes to read the story and ponder the verse, ask them to report what they discovered. Focus their comments if they do not clearly identify the sinful attitude or action.

God was not looking for a perfect king, but one after His own heart (see 1 Samuel 16—31).

Samuel was not able to find a sinless man to anoint as king of Israel. However, a man who loved and obeyed God, a man who repented and humbled himself when he sinned, that was the man that God sought (see 1 Samuel 13:14). Outward appearance did not impress God. Saul stood head and shoulders above the people, but David had a heart for God (see 16:7). David gave God glory when he defeated Goliath (see 17:1-37). David refused to oppose God's anointed king, Saul, even after Saul tried to kill him (see 19:1-18). David remained a loyal friend to Jonathan in spite of the actions of his father Saul (see 20:1-42).

Ask the group to turn to Psalm 51. This is the prayer David prayed after he sinned with Bathsheba. We will look more closely at this prayer next session. For now, ask the group to read Psalm 51 together in unison and then discuss:

What kind of heart does David describe in this prayer?

Let's list all the qualities of a person after God's own heart that is revealed in this psalm. As the group members call out the qualities you write them on a chalkboard, flipchart or overhead while they take notes on their handouts.

OPTION ONE: (FOR A 90-MINUTE SESSION)

Fighting Goliath (15 Minutes)

Say to the group: **The story of David and Goliath is more than just a great children's Sunday School story. It is a spiritual lesson on facing the problems, challenges and giants of our daily lives. Actually, two different strategies for fighting giants are described in 1 Samuel 17—David's and Saul's. We are going to divide up into pairs.**

One person in each pair will look for Saul's techniques and strategy for fighting the enemy. The other will look for David's. Share with one another what you find.

Confess some of Saul's techniques and feelings you may have used in facing challenges in your life. Also, choose one of David's techniques or attitudes that you are willing to try in future encounters with giants.

Read 2 Corinthians 10:3-6 and Ephesians 6:10-18 to one another. Then pray for one another that you will fight giants in the future with God's weapons, not your own.

SECTION TWO: GOD'S PERSON (20 MINUTES)

SAMUEL: "NAME OF GOD"

Objective: To discover through the example of Samuel's life how we can grow closer to God.

Ask everyone to spread out around the room so that they are not near anyone. Then instruct each person to silently read the prayer of Hannah in 1 Samuel 2:2-10 and the story of Samuel's encounter with God in 1 Samuel 3:1-21. Ask each person to meditate on the following statements which you have written on a chalkboard, flipchart or overhead:

One way my praise of God needs to be more like Hannah's is

_____ .

One way my relationship with God needs to be more like Samuel's is

_____ .

After giving everyone about seven minutes to meditate and reflect on these statements, invite group members to pray this litany after you. Tell them that their response is **"Lord, open my eyes to see You and my ears to hear You."**

Leader: **Lord, sometimes when You speak we don't listen.**

Group: Lord, open my eyes to see You and my ears to hear You.

Leader: **Lord, sometimes we are not looking for You or seeking Your presence.**

Group: Lord, open my eyes to see You and my ears to hear You.

Leader: **Lord, touch our eyes, our ears and most of all our hearts that we might be called people who have a heart after You.**

Group: Lord, open my eyes to see You and my ears to hear You.

OPTION TWO (FOR A 90-MINUTE SESSION)

David: A Follower of God; A Leader of Men (15 Minutes)

Refer to the large sheet of butcher paper (or a bulletin board or blank area of a wall) with the title "David: A Follower of God; A Leader of Men" written across the top.

Divide the whole group into four smaller groups. Assign each group one of the following sections of 1 Samuel:

    Group One: 1 Samuel 18; 20; 21
    Group Two: 1 Samuel 22—24
    Group Three: 1 Samuel 25—27
    Group Four: 1 Samuel 29—31

Give each group several sheets of paper and a felt-tip pen. Have each group choose a recorder. Tell them to skim their assigned chapters to find examples of David's godliness and examples of his leadership qualities. When they find each quality, they will tell their group's recorder the chapter and verse where it is located and name the example. The recorder will write down each example on a separate

sheet of paper, using large letters. Ask the group members to state their examples as briefly as possible (i.e. Trust in God—17:37; Courage—17:32).

After seven or eight minutes, ask the recorders to share their groups' examples by reading each paper as they tape them to the sheet of butcher paper (bulletin board or wall). Discuss the following:

Can you see any parallels between David's godly qualities and his leadership qualities? What are they? (His trust in God and his courage to fight; his loyalty to God and his loyalty to Saul, etc.)

Which of David's leadership qualities would the world consider unimportant or even detrimental to being a leader? (His humility, compassion, not taking advantage of his enemy, etc.)

Have a group member read 1 Samuel 15:22.

Considering some of the leaders we have studied so far, what one quality does God want from every godly leader? (Obedience to Him.) **How will you apply this to your own leadership responsibilities this week?**

Section Three: God's Son (10 Minutes)

Jesus Christ Revealed in 1 Samuel as Our King

Objective: To discover how 1 Samuel portrays Jesus Christ as our King.

Remember that before David was a king, he was a shepherd. He learned many valuable lessons about God as a shepherd. Let's form pairs and then turn to Psalm 23. With your partner go through Psalm 23 and substitute the word "Jesus" every time you see the word "Lord" or "he" in the psalm. Then read together John 10:1-21.

After the two of you have read these passages, take a piece of blank paper and write on it:

Jesus Christ my Shepherd-King is _____.

Complete the sentence. Put this paper in your Bible and read it at least once daily in the next week.

PURSUING GOD (5 MINUTES)

NEXT STEPS I NEED TO TAKE

Objective: To take a realistic assessment of one's relationship with Jesus and how that relationship might grow closer in the coming week.

Read the following list of words to the group. Ask the group members to choose one or two words that best describe their relationships with Jesus, our King, right now. Invite anyone who wishes to share the words they picked and why. Then have those who shared stand in the middle of the group and have the rest of the group pray for them either by placing their hands on their shoulders or simply forming a circle around them holding hands.

Nurtured	Fed	Anointed	Separated	Lost	Alone
Afraid	Secure	Joyful	Sad	Strong	Weak
Trusting	Doubtful	In love	Seeking	Ashamed	Forgiven

PRAYER (5 MINUTES)

SEEKING GOD'S GUIDANCE IN PRAYER

Objective: To close this session with affirmation and intercession in pairs.

Lead the pairs in praying Psalm 23 for one another. Have them pray through the psalm printed on their handouts putting their partners' names in the blanks. You can pray each phrase of the psalm and have the group members echo back that phrase putting their partners' names in the blanks.

TEACHING HELPS

Saul is anointed king but then rebels in pride (see 1 Samuel 8—15).

1 Samuel 10:8; 13:7-9 (Saul doesn't follow Samuel's instructions.)

1 Samuel 13:11,12 (Saul makes excuses instead of repenting.)

1 Samuel 13:13,14 (Saul disobeyed God.)

1 Samuel 15:1-9 (Saul disobeyed God.)

1 Samuel 15:10,11 (Saul turned away from God.)

1 Samuel 15:12 (Saul pridefully sets up a monument to himself.)

1 Samuel 15:13-19 (Saul makes excuses and blames others.)

1 Samuel 15:16-21 (Saul disobeys and does evil in God's eyes.)

1 Samuel 15:22-24 (Saul has rebelled against God.)

1 Samuel 15:25,26 (Saul feigns worship—acts religious—but has really rejected the word of God.)

1 Samuel 15:27-29 (Saul is more concerned with what man [Samuel] thinks than God.)

1 Samuel 15:30,31 (Saul wants honor or glory that belongs only to God.)

Session 10 Bible *Tuck-In*™

UNDERSTANDING 1 SAMUEL

The purpose of this session is:

- To provide an overview of 1 Samuel;
- To discover how Jesus Christ is portrayed as our King in 1 Samuel.

KEY VERSES

"But now your [Saul's] kingdom will not endure; the Lord has sought out a man after his own heart and appointed him leader of his people, because you have not kept the Lord's command." 1 Samuel 13:14

"But the Lord said to Samuel, 'Do not consider his appearance or his height, for I have rejected him. The Lord does not look at the things man looks at. Man looks at the outward appearance, but the Lord looks at the heart.'" 1 Samuel 16:7

"All those gathered here will know that it is not by sword or spear that the Lord saves; for the battle is the Lord's, and he will give all of you into our hands." 1 Samuel 17:47

SECTION ONE: GOD'S STORY (20 MINUTES)

1 SAMUEL: GOD'S NAME

— Fold —

After the two of you have read these passages, take a piece of blank paper and write on it:

Jesus Christ my Shepherd-King is _____.

- Complete the sentence. Put this paper in your Bible and read it at least once daily in the next week.

PURSUING GOD (5 MINUTES)

NEXT STEPS I NEED TO TAKE

- Read the following list of words to the group. Ask the group members to choose one or two words that best describe their relationship to Jesus, our King, right now. Invite anyone who wishes to share the words they picked and why. Then have those who shared stand in the middle of the group and have the rest of the group pray for them either by placing their hands on their shoulders or simply forming a circle around them holding hands.

Nurtured	Feed	Anointed	Separated
Lost	Alone		
Afraid	Secure	Joyful	Sad
Strong	Weak		
Trusting	Doubtful	In love	Seeking
Ashamed	Forgiven		

PRAYER (5 MINUTES)

SEEKING GOD'S GUIDANCE IN PRAYER

- Lead the pairs in praying Psalm 23 for one another. Have them pray through the psalm on their handouts putting their partners' names in the blanks. You pray each phrase of the psalm and have the group members echo back that phrase putting their partner's name in the blanks.

- Tell the group the Bible story doing the suggested activities as you come to them.
- Distribute the handout "An Overview of 1 Samuel" so group members can take notes.

OPTION ONE: (FOR A 90-MINUTE SESSION)

Fighting Goliath (15 Minutes)
- Give instructions to the group then divide into pairs and have them do the listed activity.

SECTION TWO: GOD'S PERSON (20 MINUTES)

SAMUEL: "NAME OF GOD"
- Ask everyone to spread out around the room so that they are not near anyone. Then instruct each person to silently read the prayer of Hannah in 1 Samuel 2:2-10 and the story of Samuel's encounter with God in 1 Samuel 3:1-21. Ask each person to meditate on the following statements which you have written on a chalkboard, flipchart or overhead:

One way my praise of God needs to be more like Hannah's is _____.

One way my relationship with God needs to be more like Samuel's is _____.

- After giving everyone about seven minutes to meditate and reflect on these statements, invite group members to pray this litany after you. Tell them that their response is **"Lord, open my eyes to see You and my ears to hear You."**

Leader: Lord, sometimes when You speak we don't listen.
Group: Lord, open my eyes to see You and my ears to hear You.
Leader: Lord, sometimes we are not looking for You or seeking Your presence.

Group: Lord, open my eyes to see You and my ears to hear You.
Leader: Lord, touch our eyes, our ears and most of all our hearts that we might be called people who have a heart after You.
Group: Lord, open my eyes to see You and my ears to hear You.

OPTION TWO (FOR A 90-MINUTE SESSION)

David: A Follower of God; A Leader of Men (15 Minutes)
- Divide the whole group into four smaller groups. Assign each group one of the following sections of 1 Samuel:

    Group One: 1 Samuel 18; 20; 21
    Group Two: 1 Samuel 22—24
    Group Three: 1 Samuel 25—27
    Group Four: 1 Samuel 29—31

Discuss the following:

Can you see any parallels between David's godly qualities and his leadership qualities? What are they? (His trust in God and his courage to fight; his loyalty to God and his loyalty to Saul, etc.)

Which of David's leadership qualities would the world consider unimportant or even detrimental to being a leader? (His humility, compassion, not taking advantage of his enemy, etc.)

Have a group member read 1 Samuel 15:22. What one quality does God want from every godly leader? (obedience to Him)

How will you apply this to your own leadership responsibilities this week?

SECTION THREE: GOD'S SON IN 1 SAMUEL (10 MINUTES)

JESUS CHRIST REVEALED IN 1 SAMUEL AS OUR KING
- Give instruction about Psalm 23 and John 10.

Fold

AN OVERVIEW OF 1 SAMUEL

1. 1 Samuel is dominated by three of Israel's leaders—Samuel, Saul and David.

   Notes about Samuel:

   Notes about Saul:

   Notes about David:

2. Samuel was the last of the judges, the first of the prophets, and the founder of the monarchy. (1 Samuel 1—3)

   Notes:

Revival results from:

_____   _____   _____

3. After the period of the judges, Israel was in complete cultural, spiritual and political confusion. (1 Samuel 4—7)

   Notes:

4. Saul is anointed king, but then rebels in pride. (1 Samuel 8—15)
   Saul's sinful attitudes and actions were:

   _____

   _____

   _____

   _____

   _____

   _____

5. God is not looking for a perfect king, but one after His own heart. (See 1 Samuel 16—31)

   Qualities of a person who has a heart for God:

Jesus Christ Our Shepherd-King

Put your partner's name in the blank and pray Psalm 23 for your partner:
"The LORD is _____'s shepherd; _____ shall not want.

"He maketh _____ to lie down in green pastures:
he leadeth _____ beside the still waters.

"He restoreth _____'s soul: he leadeth _____ in the paths of
righteousness for his name's sake.

"Yea, though _____ walks through the valley of the shadow of death,
_____ will fear no evil: for thou art with _____; thy rod and
thy staff they comfort _____.

"Thou preparest a table before _____ in the presence of _____'s enemies: thou anointest _____'s head with oil; _____'s cup runneth
over.

"Surely goodness and mercy shall follow _____ all the days of _____'s
life: and _____ will dwell in the house of the LORD for ever. Amen" (Psalm 23, *KJV*).

CONTINUED

Before next week's session, read:

Sunday: David Mourns for Jonathan and Saul (2 Samuel 1:1-27)

Monday: David, King of Judah (2 Samuel 2:1-32; 3:1)

Tuesday: David, King of All Israel (2 Samuel 5:1-25)

Wednesday: David's House Established (2 Samuel 11:1-27)

Thursday: David's Sin (2 Samuel 11:1-27)

Friday: David's Repentance (2 Samuel 12:1-23; Psalm 51)

Saturday: David Numbers the People (2 Samuel 24:1-17)

Understanding 2 Samuel

The purpose of this session is:
- To provide an overview of 2 Samuel;
- To discover how Jesus Christ is portrayed as our King in 2 Samuel.

In this session, group members will learn:
- Key truths about God's story in 2 Samuel;
- That Jesus Christ is revealed in 2 Samuel;
- The basic principle of being a man or woman after God's own heart;
- How to apply basic truths in 2 Samuel to their own lives.

KEY VERSES

"And the LORD said to you [David], 'You will shepherd my people Israel, and you will become their ruler.'" 2 Samuel 5:2

"'The LORD declares to you [David] that the LORD himself will establish a house for you: When your days are over and you rest with your fathers, I will raise up your offspring to succeed you, who will come from your own body, and I will establish his kingdom. He is the one who will build a house for my Name, and I will establish the throne of his kingdom forever.'" 2 Samuel 7:11-13

BEFORE THE SESSION

- Pray for group members by name asking the Holy Spirit to teach them the spiritual truths in 2 Samuel.
- Read chapter 10 in *What the Bible Is All About*.
- Prepare copies of Session 11 handout " An Overview of 2 Samuel" for every group member.
- Check off these supplies once you have secured them:
    ____ Extra Bibles, pencil and paper for group members.
- If you are having a 90-minute session, then carefully read the two option sections right now and pull together any supplies you need for them.

- Read the entire session and look up every passage. Have your Bible *Tuck-In*™ ready for yourself.
- Arrive early and be ready to warmly greet each group member as he or she arrives.
- Memorize the key verses. Share them periodically in the session and ask the group to repeat them after you.

SECTION ONE: GOD'S STORY (20 MINUTES)

2 SAMUEL: KING DAVID

Objective: To discover how God's story unfolds in 2 Samuel.

As people arrive, divide them into three sections, each subdivided into smaller groups of no more than four per group. Ask the groups in each section to take a segment of the psalms.

> Section One: Psalms 1—50
> Section Two: Psalms 51—100
> Section Three: Psalms 101—150

Ask each group to appoint a recorder and then to divide their section of the psalms equally among themselves. Have them search for the psalms of David. When they find one, jot down its number and the main theme or key verse.

After five minutes, bring the whole group back together. Let each reporter share about the psalms his or her group found and the various themes that were covered. The psalms will serve to illustrate the deep complexity and intimacy of the relationship between David and God.

Read aloud the following, doing the suggested activities as you come to them. Distribute the handout "An Overview of 2 Samuel" so group members can take notes.

The themes of 2 Samuel revolve around the life of David and his relationship with God.

At the end of 1 Samuel, Saul and Jonathan have died. David is poised first to rule Judah and then all of Israel. God establishes the throne of David forever. This Davidic covenant foreshadows the coming Anointed One—Messiah—from the household of David, who will rule forever (see 2 Samuel 7:8-17).

David as a man after God's own heart demonstrated heart qualities that bear fruit for God's work and purposes. His love for God clearly shone

through as He danced before the ark, established worship in the city of David and planned a temple for the living God.

No one in God's Word is more versatile than David. He is the shepherd boy, the court musician, the soldier, the true friend, the outcast leader, the king, the great general, the loving father, the poet, the sinner, the brokenhearted old man, yet always the lover of God.

Ask the group to think of all the heart qualities they have seen David exhibit from their overview of David to this point. As they brainstorm these qualities write them on a chalkboard, flipchart or overhead. Be certain the list includes the following:

1. Faithfulness
2. Humility
3. Patience
4. Courage
5. Big-heartedness
6. Trustfulness
7. Penitence

God blessed David. Under David's leadership, the nation was healed and united; Jerusalem was established as the spiritual and political center of Israel; Israel's enemies were defeated and peace was established within Israel and with her neighbors (see 2 Samuel 1—10).

In 2 Samuel 1—10, we see David at his best worshiping God, defeating Israel's enemies and uniting the nation.

Have the group form groups of two or three. Ask the groups to skim these chapters and on their handouts list the major accomplishments of David that they find. Then after five minutes, invite volunteers to share their findings. List them on a chalkboard, flipchart or overhead:

1. **David mourned the deaths of Saul and Jonathan (see 2 Samuel 1).**
2. **David became king over Judah and then Israel (see 2 Samuel 2—5:5).**
3. **David conquered Jerusalem and brought the ark there (see 2 Samuel 5:6—6:23).**
4. **God made a covenant with David to establish his throne forever (see 2 Samuel 7).**
5. **David expanded his kingdom geographically and solidified his rule and justice internally (see 2 Samuel 8).**
6. **David faithfully kept his covenant with Jonathan (see 2 Samuel 9).**
7. **David defeated Ammon and Aramea (see 2 Samuel 10).**

God must now deal with David's sin. As a result of his sin with Bathsheba, strife and struggles marred David's family (see 2 Samuel 11—20).

David sinned with Bathsheba and murdered her husband in an attempt to cover it. The prophet Nathan confronted David with his sin and David repented. David and Bathsheba's first child died. In his final years, David's family relationships were filled with strife, murder, incest, rebellion and division.

Ask the groups to do an overview of chapters 11—20 and to jot down under point four on their handouts all of the different things that happened to David and his family as a result of his sin with Bathsheba. As a whole group, read aloud Galatians 6:7,8 and Psalm 51:1-3,14-17. Then discuss:

What do we learn from David about forgiveness and experiencing the consequences of sin?

The last section of 2 Samuel (see chapters 21—24) give final reflections on the reign of David. His relationship with God is summarized in 23:1-7. Once again, God's everlasting covenant with David looks ahead to the coming Messiah.

One of David's final actions in 2 Samuel is to buy the future Temple site. David has a heart for worship and desires to build the Temple. God gives him the plans for the Temple, but He does not allow this man of war to build God's house. God promises that Solomon will build the Temple.

With the whole group, read 2 Samuel 23:1-7 in unison.

OPTION ONE: (FOR A 90-MINUTE SESSION)

The Anatomy of Sin and Confession (15 Minutes)

Tell the group **2 Samuel 11—12 and Psalm 51 are powerful lessons on the:**

> **Anatomy of sin.**
> **Consequences of sin.**
> **Anatomy of confession and repentance.**
> **Let's discover what these might be.**

Divide the group into pairs.

Fill out the handout entitled "Anatomy of Sin and Confession" with your partner and then we will share what we have discovered.

After sharing their findings, discuss:

How could David have avoided sin?

What can we learn from David about confession?

SECTION TWO: GOD'S PERSON (20 MINUTES)

DAVID: "BELOVED"

Objective: To discern some of David's attitudes and actions toward God that can strengthen our own relationships with God.

Divide the whole group into four or more smaller groups. Assign each group one of the following topics:

David's relationship with God;

David's relationship with his family;

David's relationship with Israel;

David's relationship with his enemies.

Each group has 10 minutes to survey 1 and 2 Samuel and find information about their topic. Each group member can skim several chapters then report back to the group. They are to summarize their information in a couple of sentences. After 10 minutes, bring the whole group back together to share what they found. Encourage the group members to take notes on what they hear. After all the groups have reported, discuss: **Many Bible characters had family problems—Adam and Eve, Noah, Abraham, Jacob, Samson, Eli, Samuel and David to mention a few. How can we avoid or minimize these problems in our own families?**

A major biblical theme emerging in David's relationships within Israel is justice. He treated his soldiers and citizens with justice and compassion. How can a government maintain both justice and compassion in our society? What should Christians do to be leaders in these areas in our culture?

OPTION TWO: (FOR A 90-MINUTE SESSION)

A Place for Worship (15 Minutes)

Ask the whole group to read 2 Samuel 24:18-25 along with you. Discuss:
What spiritual lessons about giving are to be found in this passage?
What lessons can you learn about worship?

Divide the group into groups of three or four. Ask each small group to choose a psalm of David's between Psalm 107 and 150. Ask them to read that psalm to discern an insight from David about worship. After about 10 minutes, have each group share its insight.

SECTION THREE: GOD'S SON (10 MINUTES)

JESUS CHRIST REVEALED IN 2 SAMUEL AS OUR KING

Objective: To explore God's promise to David and how it portrays our King, Jesus Christ.

Second Samuel 7:11-16 defines God's promise with David. Let's explore some other passages about this covenant: (Assign these passages for various group members to read.)

> Psalm 110
> Psalm 89:27-29
> 2 Samuel 23:3-5
> Luke 1:33
> Psalm 9:7
> Psalm 93:2
> Psalm 103:19

After reading the verses, discuss:

What do these descriptions tell us about the Son of David who will be the Messiah?

Assign these passages to be read and then discuss how Jesus is the fulfillment of this covenant: Matthew 1:1,20; 9:27; 12:23; 15:22; 20:30,31; 21:9,15; 22:42; Mark 10:47; 12:35; Luke 3:31; 18:38,39.

How is Jesus Christ revealed as the Son of David?

PURSUING GOD (5 MINUTES)

NEXT STEPS I NEED TO TAKE

Objective: To make a realistic assessment of one's relationship with Jesus and how that relationship might grow closer in the coming week.

Have the group form pairs again. Have the partners share with one another their completions to these sentences:

One quality that David had in his relationship with the Lord that I need more of is _____.

One step I will take so that my family will not experience what David's did is

_____.

PRAYER (5 MINUTES)

SEEKING GOD'S GUIDANCE IN PRAYER

Objective: To close this session with affirmation and intercession in pairs.

Have the pairs share with one another the verse from Psalm 51 that means the most to them and why.

Have the partners pray with one another by praying Psalm 51 together in unison and out loud.

Session 11 Bible *Tuck-In*™

UNDERSTANDING 2 SAMUEL

The purpose of this session is:
- To provide an overview of the contents of the book of 2 Samuel;
- To discover how Jesus Christ is revealed in 2 Samuel as our King.

KEY VERSES

"And the LORD said to you [David], 'You will shepherd my people Israel, and you will become their ruler.'" 2 Samuel 5:2

"'The LORD declares to you [David] that the LORD himself will establish a house for you: When your days are over and your rest with your fathers, I will raise up your offspring to succeed you, who will come from your own body, and I will establish his kingdom. He is the one who will build a house for my Name, and I will establish the throne of his kingdom forever.'" 2 Samuel 7:11-13

SECTION ONE: GOD'S STORY (20 MINUTES)

2 SAMUEL: KING DAVID

- Tell the group the Bible story doing the suggested activities as you come to them. Distribute the handout "Overview of 2 Samuel" so group members can take notes.

163

Fold

Psalm 103:19 Discuss as a group.

What do these descriptions tell us about the Son of David who will be the Messiah?

- Assign these passages to be read and then discuss how Jesus is the fulfillment of this covenant: Matthew 1:1,20; 9:27; 12:23; 15:22; 20:30,31; 21:9,15; 22:42; Mark 10:47; 12:35; Luke 3:31; 18:38,39.
Discuss:

How is Jesus Christ revealed as the Son of David?

PURSUING GOD (5 MINUTES)

NEXT STEPS I NEED TO TAKE

- Put the group back into pairs. Have the partners share with one another the completion to these sentences:

The one quality that David had in His relationship with the Lord that I need more of is _____

The one step I will take so that my family will not experience what David's did is _____

PRAYER (5 MINUTES)

SEEKING GOD'S GUIDANCE IN PRAYER

- Have the pairs share with one another which verse in Psalm 51 means the most to them and why.
- Have the pairs now pray with one another by praying Psalm 51 together in unison and out loud.

OPTION ONE: (FOR A 90-MINUTE SESSION)

The Anatomy of Sin and Confession (15 Minutes)

• Divide the group into pairs.

• Tell them to Fill out the section of the handout entitled "Anatomy of Sin and Confession" with your partner and then we will share what we have discovered.

Discuss:

How could David have avoided sin?

What can we learn from David about confession?

SECTION TWO: GOD'S PERSON (20 MINUTES)

DAVID: BELOVED

• Divide the whole group into four smaller groups. Assign each group one of these topics:

David's Relationship with God;

David's Relationship with Absalom;

David's Relationship with Israel;

David's Relationship with his enemies.

• Each group has 10 minutes to survey 1 and 2 Samuel to find information about their topic. They are then to summarize their information into a couple of sentences. After 10 minutes, bring the groups back together to share with the whole group what they found. Encourage the group members to take notes on what they hear. After all the groups have reported, discuss the following:

Many of our Bible characters have had family problems—Adam and Eve, Noah, Abraham, Jacob, Samson, Eli, Samuel and David to mention a few. What unique difficulties do Christian leaders face in relating to wives and children? How

can we avoid these problems in our own families?

A major biblical theme emerging in David's relationships within Israel is justice. He treated his soldiers and citizens with justice and compassion. How can government maintain both justice and compassion in our society? What should Christians do to be leaders in these areas in our culture?

OPTION TWO: (FOR A 90-MINUTE SESSION)

A Place for Worship (15 Minutes)

• Ask the whole group to read 2 Samuel 24:18-25 along with you.

Discuss:

What spiritual lessons are to be found in this passage about giving?

What lessons are there about worship?

• With the whole group look through Psalms 107 to 150. Stop at each psalm that was written by David and is focused on worship. Write the main theme of that psalm on a chalkboard, flipchart or overhead and then go to the next. When you have completed this survey, you will have an overview of David's heart for worship.

Look over the list and discuss:

Which of these worship themes are most important to us in personal worship?

Which of these themes need to be more present in our corporate worship?

SECTION THREE: GOD'S SON (10 MINUTES)

JESUS CHRIST REVEALED IN 2 SAMUEL AS OUR KING

• Assign these passages for group members to read: Psalm 110; Psalm 89:19-37; 2 Samuel 23:3-5; Luke 1:33; Psalm 9:7; Psalm 93:2;

An Overview of 2 Samuel

1   The themes of 2 Samuel revolve around the life of David and his relationship with God.

   Notes:

2.   David as a man after God's own heart demonstrates heart qualities that bear fruit for God's work and purposes. His love for God clearly shines through as he dances before the ark, establishes worship in the city of David and plans a Temple for the living God.

   Notes:

3.   God blesses David. Under David's leadership, the nation was healed and united; Jerusalem was established as the spiritual and political center of Israel; Israel's enemies were defeated and peace was established within Israel and with her neighbors (see 2 Samuel 1—10).

   Notes:

4.   God must now deal with David's sin. 2 Samuel 11—20 chronicle the strife and struggles of David's family as a result of sinning with Bathsheba.

   Notes:

CONTINUED

5. The last section of 2 Samuel (chapters 21—24) give final reflections on the reign of David. One summary of David's relationship with God can be found in 23:1-7. Once again, the everlasting covenant with David is highlighted looking ahead to the coming Messiah.

Notes:

ANATOMY OF SIN AND CONFESSION

1. Read 2 Samuel 11. List the sins that David committed:

   2 Samuel 11:1 _____

   2 Samuel 11:2 _____

   2 Samuel 11:4,5 _____

   2 Samuel 11:6-13 _____

   2 Samuel 11:14-24 _____

   2 Samuel 11:14-17, 25 _____

2. Read 2 Samuel 12. Describe David's repentance and the consequences of his sin.

3. Read Psalm 51. List all the ways David confessed and all that God desires.

   Confession   God Desires

CONTINUED

Before next week's session, read:

Sunday: Building and Dedicating the Temple (1 Kings 6:1-14; 8:22-53)

Monday: Solomon's Glorious Reign (1 Kings 10:1-29)

Tuesday: The Kingdom Divided (1 Kings 12:1-13)

Wednesday: The Prophet Elijah (1 Kings 17:1—18:46)

Thursday: Elijah and Elisha (2 Kings 2:1-22)

Friday: The Captivity of Israel (The Northern Kingdom) (2 Kings 17:7-23)

Saturday: The Captivity of Judah (The Southern Kingdom) (2 Kings 25:1-21)

Understanding Kings and Chronicles

The purpose of this session is:
- To provide an overview of Kings and Chronicles;
- To discover how Jesus Christ is portrayed as our King in these books.

In this session, group members will learn:
- Key truths about God's story in the books of the Kings and Chronicles;
- That these books portray Jesus Christ as our King;
- The basic principle that rejection of God leads to destruction;
- How to apply basic truths in these books to their own lives.

KEY VERSES

"'I [David] am about to go the way of all the earth,'" he said [to Solomon]. "'"So be strong, show yourself a man, and observe what the LORD your God requires: Walk in his ways, and keep his decrees and commands, his laws and requirements, as written in the Law of Moses, so that you may prosper in all you do and wherever you go." 1 Kings 2:2,3

"In those days the LORD began to reduce the size of Israel." 2 Kings 10:32

BEFORE THE SESSION

- Pray for group members by name asking the Holy Spirit to teach them the spiritual truths in Kings and Chronicles.
- Read chapter 11 in *What the Bible Is All About.*
- Prepare copies of Session 12 handouts "An Overview of Kings and Chronicles" and "The Temple and the Tabernacle" for every group member.
- Check off these supplies once you have secured them:
    - ____ Have extra Bible, pencils and paper for group members.
    - ____ Have an inexpensive cup you can break and a nonbreakable dish that would be very difficult to break even if dropped.
    - ____ Get an old sheet that will rip easily.

- If you are having a 90-minute session, then carefully read the two option sections right now and pull together any supplies you need for them.
- Read the entire session and look up every passage. Have your Bible *Tuck-In*™ ready for yourself.
- Arrive early and be ready to warmly greet each group member as he or she arrives.
- Memorize the key verses. Share them periodically in the session and ask the group to repeat them after you.

SECTION ONE: GOD'S STORY (25 MINUTES)

THE BOOKS OF KINGS AND CHRONICLES

Objective: To see how God's story unfolds in the books of Kings and Chronicles.

The historical period of 1 and 2 Chronicles roughly parallels 1 and 2 Kings. Kings emphasizes the role of the kings while Chronicles looks at the same period from the perspective of worship.

Read aloud the following, doing the suggested activities as you come to them. Distribute the handout "An Overview of Kings and Chronicles" so group members can take notes.

God blessed Solomon with wisdom, power and wealth making Israel one of the greatest kingdoms of the world (see 1 Kings 1—10)!

In a dream, God asked Solomon what he desired. Solomon asked for wisdom. With wisdom came prosperity, wealth and peace. Under his rule, Israel expanded to the boundaries God had intended in the conquest of the Promised Land. Solomon builds one of the wonders of the ancient world—the Temple—for God.

Give everyone in the group a copy of the Sessio 12 handout, "The Temple and the Tabernacle." With the whole group look at the two pictures and discuss:
What are some of the major similarities between the Temple and the Tabernacle?

With wealth and power came the temptations of pride and abuse. Solomon gave in to both. He married foreign wives and built temples to their idols. His building projects and expansion overtaxed and burdened his people (see 1 Kings 11).

Jeroboam, his general, rebelled and fled from his court. He became the king of the Northern Kingdom of Israel after Solomon's death.

Read this text to the whole group.

"As Solomon grew old, his wives turned his heart after other gods, and his heart was not fully devoted to the LORD his God, as the heart of David his father had been. He followed Ashtoreth the goddess of the Sidonians, and Molech the detestable god of the Ammonites. So Solomon did evil in the eyes of the LORD; he did not follow the LORD completely, as David his father had done. The LORD became angry with Solomon because his heart had turned away from the LORD, the God of Israel, who had appeared to him twice" (1 Kings 11:4-6,9).

Discuss the following:

Why do you think Solomon turned away from God?

What can keep us from experiencing the same destiny as Solomon?

After Solomon's death, the kingdoms divided. Jeroboam reigned over the ten tribes of the Northern Kingdom, Israel. Solomon's son, Rehoboam, ruled Judah, the Southern Kingdom (see 1 Kings 12—16).

To keep his people from moving south, Jeroboam set up golden calves at Bethel and Dan. Often he is called in the Bible the one who made Israel sin (see 1 Kings 16:2). Sin, wickedness, luxury and corruption ruled in Israel.

Take an old sheet and tear it into 12 pieces. Give twelve different people the pieces of the sheet and then read 1 Kings 11:29-40. Then say, **Ten tribes were given to the Northern Kingdom. By this time, the tribe of Benjamin had been assimilated into the tribe of Judah representing one tribe.**

The prophet Elijah was the strength of Israel. He stood firm in the midst of the terror employed by Ahab and Jezebel. He confronted the wickedness of their court as well as the prophets of Baal on Mount Carmel .

In 732 B.C., God's judgment was exacted when Assyria carried the Northern Kingdom of Israel into exile. The 10 tribes were scattered and lost (see 1 Kings 17—2 Kings 17).

Take an inexpensive coffee cup. Throw it down and watch it shatter. (Caution: Do not throw it near anyone as pieces may fly!) Now take a nonbreakable dish. Throw it down. It will bounce and not break. Try to carefully pick up the pieces of the cup and put them back together. Obviously, that is an impossible task. Then say to the group:

The cup represents Israel—shattered and broken—which was lost in the Assyrian empire. The dish is Judah. In exile for a season, she stayed together and God brought her back for an eternal purpose—out of Judah would come the Messiah.

In 586 B.C., God used Babylon to carry Judah into exile. However, the Jews were not scattered throughout the empire and were allowed to

return to rebuild the Temple and Jerusalem (see 2 Kings 18—25).

God was using even the rulers of foreign nations to work out His plan. Cyrus, king of Persia, issued a decree allowing the Jews to return to their homeland.

The Southern Kingdom had periods of faithfulness to God when temple worship would be revived and people would forsake idolatry and seek God once again. These revivals usually came through the faithfulness of a righteous king.

Have everyone find a partner. Tell the pairs that they are to look up each of the passages about revival that are listed on their handouts and to complete that section with their partners.

OPTION ONE: (FOR A 90-MINUTE SESSION)

Rulers of Israel (15 Minutes)

Write the following rulers on a chalkboard, flipchart or overhead:

Jeroboam (See 1 Kings 12:25—14:20)

Ahab (See 1 Kings 16:29—22:40)

Ahaziah (See 1 Kings 22:51—2 Kings 1:18)

Jehu (See 2 Kings 9:30—10:36)

Jehoash (See 2 Kings 13:10-25)

Divide into five groups. Assign one king to each group. Give everyone about five minutes to look up the king and read about his reign.

Write the following questions on a chalkboard, flipchart or overhead and ask each group to give a short report to the whole group on the king they have researched. Ask the group members to focus their studies on answering these questions:

How did this king lead Israel into doing evil?

How did God respond to this king?

What consequences did this king suffer?

After this discussion, with the whole group discuss:

As a whole, in what ways did the kings of the Northern Kingdom lead Israel to do evil in God's eyes?

How does God handle apostasy in the lives of His people?

What similarities are there between Israel and our culture?

SECTION TWO: GOD'S PERSON (15 MINUTES)

ELIJAH AND ELISHA: GOD'S PROPHETS

Objective: To understand how God used these mighty prophets for His purposes.

Briefly tell the story of 1 Kings 18—19. On a chalkboard, flipchart or overhead write these two titles:

Elijah—Mighty Prophet   Elijah—Fearful Man

As a group, list all the God-given qualities Elijah possessed in 1 Kings 18 and all the weak, human qualities he exhibited in 1 Kings 19. Discuss:

Why do periods of depression seem to follow great spiritual victories?

What did God do to bring Elijah out of his depressed state?

What does God do in our lives to lift us up when we are down?

Now ask everyone to turn to 2 Kings 2—8:6. Have the group help you make a list of all the miracles God did through Elisha. Now discuss:

What are the primary differences that you see between the prophetic ministries of Elijah and Elisha? (Some of the differences that the group might see are that Elijah was the prophet of judgment, law and severity, and Elisha was the prophet of grace, love and tenderness.)

How did God use these prophets to rebuke and discipline Israel?

OPTION TWO: (FOR A 90-MINUTE SESSION)

Rulers of Judah (15 Minutes)

Write the following rulers on a chalkboard, flipchart or overhead:

Rehoboam (See 1 Kings 12:1-24; 14:21-31)

Joash (See 2 Kings 12)

Ahaz (See 2 Kings 16)

Hezekiah (See 2 Kings 18—20:21)

Jehoiakim (See 2 Kings 23:34—24:7)

Divide into five groups. Assign one king to each group. Give everyone about five minutes to look up the king and read about his reign.

Write the following questions on a chalkboard, flipchart or overhead and ask each group to give a short report to the whole group on the king they have researched. Ask the group members to focus their studies on answering these questions:

What did this king do to lead Judah toward or away from God?

How did this king relate to God?

After everyone has reported on the kings they researched, discuss the following:

Why do you think God did not deal as harshly with Judah as He did with Israel?

How does a righteous leader influence a whole nation toward righteousness?

What could our culture learn from ancient Judah and her rulers?

Section Three: God's Son (10 Minutes)

Jesus Christ Revealed as Our King

Objective: To see how Solomon's rule relates to Jesus Christ's rule.

The lessons of Israel are important lessons for the Church. Just as Israel could only be strong and united under one king, so the Church is strong and united under our King Jesus. Sin always brings division. Sin in Solomon's life brought division in Israel. Sin in the Church brings divisions. With the whole group, discuss the qualities of Solomon's reign that foreshadow the reign of the King of kings. Then discuss the qualities of Solomon's reign that led to the division of the kingdom. Your discussion will include some of the following:

Solomon Was a Wise and Good King

1. He had a spiritual upbringing under the righteous Nathan (see 2 Samuel 12:25).
2. The kingdom rejoiced when he sat on the throne (see 1 Kings 1:46).
3. His charge from his father was full of promise (see 1 Kings 2:1-9).
4. His wisdom was from God (see 1 Kings 3).
5. His work was building a temple to worship God.
6. His reign was filled with wealth and glory.
7. He was filled with love and affection.

Solomon's Sins

1. He dealt cruelly with his brother Adonijah (see 1 Kings 2:24-25).
2. His heart was filled with pride (see 1 Kings 10:18-29).
3. He married hundreds of foreign women (see 1 Kings 11).
4. He fell into idolatry (see 1 Kings 11).
5. He did evil in God's eyes.

PURSUING GOD (5 MINUTES)

NEXT STEPS I NEED TO TAKE

Objective: To apply lessons learned from Solomon and Elijah.

In pairs, share the completion to these sentences:

The most important lesson I learned from the life of Solomon was

_____.

The most important lesson I learned from Elijah's life was

_____.

PRAYER (5 MINUTES)

SEEKING GOD'S GUIDANCE IN PRAYER

Objective: To close this session with affirmation and intercession in pairs.

Solomon accomplished great things for God but also fell tragically into idolatry. First Kings 3:3 gives us a clue early on that Solomon will have problems: "Solomon showed his love for the Lord by walking according to the statutes of his father David, except that he offered sacrifices and burned incense on the high places." As you remember from Gideon's life, the high places were where idolatry was practiced by the Canaanites.

Ask the group, What is the "except" in your life? Are you following God in almost every way except one or two? Take a few moments to confess to the Lord any exceptions in your life. Pray for His forgiveness and courage to remove the "excepts" from your life.

Session 12 Bible *Tuck-In*™

UNDERSTANDING THE BOOKS OF THE KINGS AND CHRONICLES

The purpose of this session is:

- To provide an overview of Kings and Chronicles;
- To discover how Jesus Christ is portrayed as our King in these books.

KEY VERSES

"'I [David] am about to go the way of all the earth," he said [to Solomon]. "So be strong, show yourself a man, and observe what the LORD your God requires: Walk in his ways, and keep his decrees and commands, his laws and requirements, as written in the Law of Moses, so that you may prosper in all you do and wherever you go.'" 1 Kings 2:2,3

"In those days the LORD began to reduce the size of Israel." 2 Kings 10:32

SECTION ONE: GOD'S STORY (25 MINUTES)

THE BOOKS OF KINGS AND CHRONICLES

- Tell the group the Bible story doing the suggested activities as

- Fold -

175

What did this king do to lead Judah toward God or away from God?

How did this king relate to God?

After everyone has reported on the king they researched, discuss the listed:

SECTION THREE: GOD'S SON (10 MINUTES)

JESUS CHRIST REVEALED AS OUR KING

- The lessons of Israel are important lessons for the Church. Just as Israel could only be strong and united under one king, so the Church is strong and united under our King Jesus. Sin always brings division. Sin in Solomon's life brought division in Israel. Sin in the Church brings divisions.

- With the whole group, discuss the qualities of Solomon's reign that foreshadow the reign of the King of kings. Then discuss the qualities of Solomon's reign that led to the division of the kingdom.

PURSUING GOD (5 MINUTES)

NEXT STEPS I NEED TO TAKE

- In pairs, share the completion to these sentences:

The most important lesson I learned from the life of Solomon was _____

The most important lesson I learned from Elijah's life was _____

PRAYER (5 MINUTES)

SEEKING GOD'S GUIDANCE IN PRAYER

- Read 1 Kings 3:3 to the group and then close in silent prayer as they meditate on the "excepts" in their lives.

you come to them. Distribute the handout "An Overview of Kings and Chronicles" so group members can take notes.

OPTION ONE: (FOR A 90-MINUTE SESSION)

Rulers of Israel (15 Minutes)

• Write the following rulers on a chalkboard, flipchart or overhead:
Jeroboam (See 1 Kings 12:25—14:20)
Ahab (See 1 Kings 16:29—22:40)
Ahaziah (See 1 Kings 22:51—2 Kings 1:18)
Jehu (See 2 Kings 9:30—10:36)
Jehoash (See 2 Kings 13:10-25)

• Divide into five groups. Assign one king to each group. Give everyone about five minutes to look up the king and read about his reign.

• Write the following questions on a chalkboard, flipchart or overhead and ask each group to give a short report to the whole group on the king they have researched. Ask the group members to focus their studies on answering these questions:

How did this king lead Israel into doing evil?
How did God respond to this king?
What consequences did this king suffer?

After this discussion, with the whole group discuss the listed questions:

SECTION TWO: GOD'S PERSON (15 MINUTES)

ELIJAH AND ELISHA: GOD'S PROPHETS

• Briefly tell the story of 1 Kings 18—19. On a chalkboard, flipchart or overhead write these two titles for lists:

Elijah—Mighty Prophet   Elijah—Fearful Man

• As a group, list all the God-given qualities Elijah possessed in

---Fold---

1 Kings 18 and all the weak, human qualities he exhibited in 1 Kings 19. Discuss:

What did God do to bring Elijah out of his depressed state?
What does God do in our lives to lift us up when we are down?

Why do periods of depression seem to follow great spiritual victories?

• Now ask everyone to turn to 2 Kings 2—8:6. Have the group help you make a list of all the miracles God did through Elisha. Now discuss:

What are the primary differences that you see between the prophetic ministries of Elijah and Elisha? (Some of the differences that the group might see are that Elijah was the prophet of judgment, law and severity, and Elisha was the prophet of grace, love and tenderness.)
How did God use these prophets to rebuke and discipline Israel?

OPTION TWO: (FOR A 90-MINUTE SESSION)

Rulers of Judah (15 Minutes)

• Write the following rulers on a chalkboard, flipchart or overhead:
Rehoboam (See 1 Kings 12:1-24; 14:21-31)
Joash (See 2 Kings 12)
Ahaz (See 2 Kings 16)
Hezekiah (See 2 Kings 18—20:21)
Jehoiakim (See 2 Kings 23:34—24:7)

• Divide into five groups. Assign one king to each group. Give everyone about five minutes to look up the king and read about his reign.

• Write the following questions on a chalkboard, flipchart or overhead and ask each group to give a short report to the whole group on the king they have researched. Ask the group members to focus their studies on answering these questions:

AN OVERVIEW OF KINGS AND CHRONICLES

1. God blessed Solomon with wisdom, power and wealth making Israel one of the greatest kingdoms of the world! (see 1 Kings 1—10)

   Notes:

2. With wealth and power comes the temptations of pride and abuse. Solomon gave into both. He married countless foreign wives and built temples to their idols. His building projects and expansion overtaxed and burdened his people. (see 1 Kings 11)

   Notes:

3. After Solomon's death, the kingdoms divided. Jeroboam reigned over the ten tribes of the Northern Kingdom, Israel. Solomon's son, Rehoboam, ruled Judah, the Southern Kingdom. (see 1 Kings 12—16)

   Notes:

4. In 732 B.C., God's judgment was exacted when Assyria carried the Northern Kingdom of Israel into exile. The 10 tribes were scattered and lost. (see 1 Kings 17—2 Kings 17)

   Notes:

CONTINUED

5. In 586 B.C., God used Babylon to carry Judah into exile. However, the Jews were not scattered throughout the empire and were allowed to return to rebuild the Temple and Jerusalem. (see 2 Kings 18—25)

Notes:

2 CHRONICLES—A BOOK OF REVIVALS!

The Scripture	The King	What Happened in the Revival?
1. 2 Chronicles 15	_____	_____
2. 2 Chronicles 20	_____	_____
3. 2 Chronicles 23—24	_____	_____
4. 2 Chronicles 29—31	_____	_____
5. 2 Chronicles 25	_____	_____

Before next week's session, read:
Sunday: Jews Return to Jerusalem (Ezra 1—3)
Monday: Discouragement and Joy (Ezra 4—6)
Tuesday: Ezra's Expedition (Ezra 7—10)
Wednesday: Nehemiah Rebuilds the Wall (Nehemiah 1—3)
Thursday: Overcoming Opposition (Nehemiah 4—6)
Friday: Nehemiah Rebuilds the Morals (Nehemiah 7—9)
Saturday: Reforming Through Spiritual Faith (Nehemiah 11—13)

The Temple and the Tabernacle

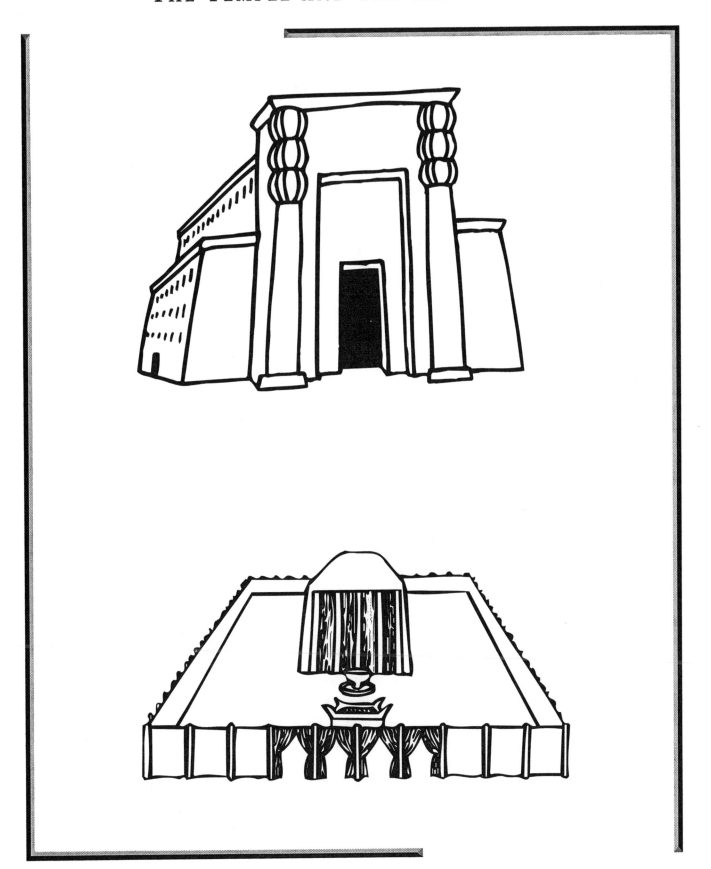

Understanding Ezra, Nehemiah and Esther

The purpose of this session is:
- To provide an overview of Ezra, Nehemiah and Esther;
- To discover how Jesus Christ is portrayed as our Restorer in Ezra and Nehemiah.

In this session, group members will learn:
- Key truths about God's story in Ezra, Nehemiah and Esther;
- That the books of Ezra and Nehemiah portray Jesus as our Restorer;
- The basic principle of God's mercy and restoration;
- How to apply basic truths in Scripture to their own lives.

KEY VERSES

"Do not think that because you are in the king's house you alone of all the Jews will escape. For if you remain silent at this time, relief and deliverance for the Jews will arise from another place, but you and your father's family will perish. And who knows but that you have come to royal position for such a time as this?" Esther 4:13,14

"But now, for a brief moment, the LORD our God has been gracious in leaving us a remnant and giving us a firm place in his sanctuary, and so our God gives light to our eyes and a little relief in our bondage. Though we are slaves, our God has not deserted us in our bondage. He has shown us kindness in the sight of the kings of Persia: He has granted us new life to rebuild the house of our God and repair its ruins, and he has given us a wall of protection in Judah and Jerusalem." Ezra 9:8,9

"Remember the instruction you gave your servant Moses, saying, 'If you are unfaithful, I will scatter you among the nations, but if you return to me and obey my commands, then even if your exiled people are at the farthest horizon, I will gather them from there and bring them to the place I have chosen as a dwelling for my Name.'" Nehemiah 1:8,9

BEFORE THE SESSION

- Pray for group members by name asking the Holy Spirit to teach them the spiritual truths in Ezra, Nehemiah and Esther.
- Read chapters 12 and 14 in *What the Bible Is All About*.
- Prepare copies of Session 13 handouts "An Overview of Ezra, Nehemiah and Esther" for every group member.
- Check off these supplies once you have secured them:
  ___ Have extra Bibles, pencils and papers for all the group members.
- If you are having a 90-minute session, then carefully read the two option sections right now and pull together any supplies you need for them.
- Read the entire session and look up every passage. Have your Bible *Tuck-In*™ ready for yourself.
- Arrive early and be ready to warmly greet each group member as he or she arrives.
- Memorize the key verses. Share them periodically in the session and ask the group to repeat them after you.

SECTION ONE: GOD'S STORY (20 MINUTES)

EZRA, NEHEMIAH AND ESTHER: THE RESCUE, RETURN AND RESTORATIONS

Objective: To provide an overview of how the Bible portrays Jesus Christ as our Restorer.

Read aloud the following, doing the suggested activities as you come to them. Distribute the handout "An Overview of Ezra, Nehemiah and Esther" so group members can take notes.

The purposes of God may sometimes seem delayed, but they are never abandoned. Judah was in exile, but not lost. God was disciplining His people, not abandoning them! Through the courage and faith of Mordecai and Esther, God saved His people from extinction (see Esther 1—9).

The books of Ezra and Nehemiah tell the story of how God remembered His people and brought them back from exile. Esther tells how God saved His people

from extinction while they were in exile.

Have everyone in the group read Jeremiah 29:10-13. This passage tells God's plan for Israel in exile and beyond.

As the book of Ezra opens, Cyrus, king of Persia, makes a proclamation permitting the Jews to return to Jerusalem (see Ezra 1—2).

God had spoken this prophetic truth 200 years before this time through the prophet Isaiah (see Isaiah 44:28; 45:1-4). Cyrus gave back to Zerubbabel the golden vessels which Nebuchadnezzar had taken from the Temple. Upon returning, Ezra and the Jews first laid the foundation and then built an altar to God (see Ezra 3:2).

Explain to the group that a prophet, *nabi* in the Hebrew, means "voice piece or spokesman." The Old Testament prophet foretold and told forth God's Word. Discuss with the whole group:

How did the Jews know when a prophet was truly speaking God's Word? (Negatively, if it didn't happen like a prophet said, he or she couldn't be a prophet of God. Positively, if it did happen like a prophet said, that was good but not a guarantee of prophetic authenticity. If they waited many years and a prophecy was fulfilled, this was a clear case that God knew the future.)

How does God still use people to speak His Word today?

Under the priest Ezra, observing the law and restoring temple sacrifice and worship were reestablished. Though the returning Jews faced many obstacles, they persevered in building the Temple and observing God's law (see Ezra 3—10).

Ezra 7:10 (*KJV*) states that Ezra "prepared his heart to seek the law of the LORD, and to do it, and to teach in Israel statutes and judgments."

One of the difficult problems faced by the returning Jews was that of intermarriage (see Ezra 9—10). God kept His people Israel separate and holy unto Him through worship, circumcision, giving them a land in which to live and the Law and the Temple for living and worshiping.

Discuss:

How can we prepare our hearts for the worship of God and the teaching of His Word? Why do you suppose God didn't want the Jews to intermarry? What problems does the marriage of a Christian and nonbeliever cause today? What would you say to your children if they wished to date or to marry an unbeliever? (Note 2 Corinthians 6:14.)

God inspired Nehemiah to return to Jerusalem to repair the walls and rebuild the city. Of course, he faced opposition from the Samaritans who had not gone into exile (see Nehemiah 1—13).

Not only did Nehemiah have to repair the walls and the city, he had to repair the

people's morals. He had the law read publicly and explained to the people. (See Nehemiah 8:1-13.)

OPTION ONE: (FOR A 90-MINUTE SESSION)

Nehemiah: Godly Leadership (15 Minutes)

Say to the group: **Nehemiah exhibited godly leadership in returning to Jerusalem to rebuild the walls and restore a holy lifestyle to the Jews.**

Ask the group to skim through the book of Nehemiah with you. Discover as a group the qualities of godliness and holiness you see in Nehemiah. List these qualities on a chalkboard, flipchart or overhead. Ask the group members to prioritize the importance of these qualities from the most to the least important for godly leaders today.

SECTION TWO: GOD'S PERSON (20 MINUTES)

ESTHER: "FOR SUCH A TIME AS THIS"

Objective: To understand how Esther's qualities as a godly leader can be applied in our own lives.

Divide the whole group into five smaller groups. Assign each group one of these sections from Esther:

> Group 1: Rejection of Vashti (see Esther 1)
> Group 2: Crowning of Esther (see Esther 2)
> Group 3: Plotting of Haman (see Esther 3—4)
> Group 4: Venture of Esther (see Esther 5)
> Group 5: Deliverance of the Jews (see Esther 6—10)

Tell them that their job is to role-play what happened in their section. They can either have a narrator, they can mime or they can act out the story with speaking parts. Give the groups ten minutes to put their plays together.

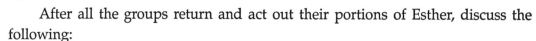

After all the groups return and act out their portions of Esther, discuss the following:

How was this persecution of the Jews similar to the holocaust?

How was it different?

Why have the Jews been persecuted through the centuries?

How can we as Christians build loving relationships with the Jews in our culture?

OPTION TWO: (FOR A 90-MINUTE SESSION)

Ezra: Public Worship and Confession (15 Minutes)

Read Ezra 10:1-4 and Nehemiah 8:1-3,5,6 to the whole group. Then divide the group into four smaller ones. Ask them to read Ezra 9—10 and Nehemiah 8—9. Have one person in each small group write down everything the group learns about prayer, worship and learning God's Word in these chapters. After seven minutes, gather the whole group back together.

Ask one person from each group to report what his or her group has learned. List these things on a chalkboard, flipchart or overhead as the groups report. Then discuss the following with the whole group:

What did the ancient Jews do in prayer and worship that we should be doing?

What keeps us from doing these things?

SECTION THREE: GOD'S SON (10 MINUTES)

JESUS CHRIST REVEALED AS OUR RESTORER

Objective: To understand how these books portray Jesus Christ as our Restorer.

Remember that God always keeps His promises. As Nehemiah knew, God would keep His promise to restore His people if they repented and returned to Him. God promised a coming Messiah who would restore peace, prosperity and the kingdom to Israel (see 2 Samuel 7:16). God would also restore the Davidic line to the throne of Israel. The Bible portrays Jesus as our Restorer. The Savior heals,

restores and frees His people from sin and bondage.

Ask everyone to find a partner. Ask the partners to share answers to the following:

When Israel returned from exile, what did God restore?

In Jesus, what did God restore to His people?

In Jesus, what has been restored in your life?

Invite the partners to share what Jesus has restored in their personal lives or their families' lives. Then gather the whole group back together. Have a praise time in which every person completes this sentence:

I praise Jesus for restoring _____.

Have the whole group see how many of the answers for the following blanks they can guess. They can fill them in on their handouts. After a few minutes, go through the list and share the answers. Then have them repeat each completed statement one or two more times to anchor this Old Testament survey of how Jesus Christ is portrayed.

> Genesis portrays Jesus Christ as <u>our Creator-God.</u>
> Exodus portrays Jesus Christ as <u>our Passover Lamb.</u>
> Leviticus portrays Jesus Christ as <u>our Sacrifice for sin.</u>
> Numbers portrays Jesus Christ as <u>our "Lifted-Up One."</u>
> Deuteronomy portrays Jesus Christ as <u>our true Prophet.</u>
> Joshua portrays Jesus Christ as <u>Captain of our salvation.</u>
> Judges portrays Jesus Christ as <u>our Deliverer-Judge.</u>
> Ruth portrays Jesus Christ as <u>our Kinsman-Redeemer.</u>
> First and 2 Samuel, Kings and Chronicles all portray Jesus Christ as <u>our King.</u>
> Ezra and Nehemiah portray Jesus Christ as <u>our Restorer.</u>

PURSUING GOD (5 MINUTES)

NEXT STEPS I NEED TO TAKE

Objective: To take a realistic assessment of one's relationship with Jesus and how that relationship might grow closer in the coming week.

Ask group members to form pairs again. Say, **Meditate on what God needs to rebuild and restore:**

> **Your relationship with God.**
> **Your relationship with family.**
> **Your relationship with someone at work or school.**
> **Your relationship with someone in the church.**
> **Your relationship with an enemy.**

Invite the pairs to share about one of these with each other and then to pray for one another.

PRAYER (5 MINUTES)

SEEKING GOD'S GUIDANCE IN PRAYER

Objective: To have confession and intercession for our nation as Ezra did in his day.

In Ezra 9, Ezra prays on behalf of the sins of God's people. Ask the group members to write a prayer of confession for our nation on their handouts. In closing, invite group members to share the prayers that they have written with everyone.

Session 13 Bible *Tuck-In™*

UNDERSTANDING EZRA, NEHEMIAH AND ESTHER

The purpose of this session is:

- To provide an overview of Ezra, Nehemiah and Esther;
- To discover how Jesus Christ is revealed in these books as our Restorer.

KEY VERSES

"Do not think that because you are in the king's house you alone of all the Jews will escape. For if you remain silent at this time, relief and deliverance for the Jews will arise from another place, but you and your father's family will perish. And who knows but that you have come to royal position for such a time as this?" Esther 4:13,14

"But now, for a brief moment, the LORD our God has been gracious in leaving us a remnant and giving us a firm place in his sanctuary, and so our God gives light to our eyes and a little relief in our bondage. Though we are slaves, our God has not deserted us in our bondage. He has shown us kindness in the sight of the kings of Persia: He has granted us new life to rebuild the house of our God and repair its ruins, and he has given us a wall of protection in Judah and Jerusalem." Ezra 9:8,9

SECTION THREE: GOD'S SON (10 MINUTES)

JESUS CHRIST REVEALED AS OUR RESTORER

- Ask everyone to find a partner. Ask the partners to share answers to the following:

  When Israel returned from exile, what did God restore?

  In Jesus, what did God restore to His people?

  In Jesus, what has been restored in your life?

- Invite the partners to share what Jesus has restored in their personal lives or their families' lives. Then gather the whole group back together. Have a praise time as we read about in Nehemiah in which every person completes this sentence:

  I praise Jesus for restoring _____.

- As a whole group, see how many of the blanks they can guess. They can fill them in on their handouts. Then recite the list one or two more times to anchor this Old Testament survey of how Jesus is portrayed.

PURSUING GOD (5 MINUTES)

NEXT STEPS I NEED TO TAKE

  Your relationship with an enemy.

- Invite the pairs to share about one of these with each other and then to pray for one another.

PRAYER (5 MINUTES)

SEEKING GOD'S GUIDANCE IN PRAYER

- In Ezra 9, Ezra prays on behalf of the sins of God's people. Ask each group member to write a prayer of confession for our nation on their handouts. In closing, invite group members to share the prayers that they have written with the whole group.

"Remember the instruction you gave your servant Moses, saying, 'If you are unfaithful, I will scatter you among the nations, but if you return to me and obey my commands, then even if your exiled people are at the farthest horizon, I will gather them from there and bring them to the place I have chosen as a dwelling for my Name.'"
Nehemiah 1:8,9

SECTION ONE: GOD'S STORY (20 MINUTES)

EZRA, NEHEMIAH, ESTHER: THE RESCUE, RETURN AND RESTORATION

• Tell the group the Bible story doing the suggested activities as you come to them. Distribute the handout "An Overview of Ezra, Nehemiah and Esther" so group members can take notes.

OPTION ONE: (FOR A 90-MINUTE SESSION)

Nehemiah: Godly Leadership (15 Minutes)

• Ask the group to skim through the book of Nehemiah with you. Discover as a group the qualities of godliness and holiness you see in Nehemiah. List these qualities on a chalkboard, flipchart or overhead. Ask the group members to prioritize the importance of these qualities from the most important to the least for godly leaders today. Then discuss the listed questions.

SECTION TWO: GOD'S PERSON (20 MINUTES)

ESTHER: "FOR SUCH A TIME AS THIS."

• Divide the whole group into five smaller groups. Assign each group one of these sections from Esther:

Group 1: Rejection of Vashti (see Esther 1);
Group 2: Crowning of Esther (see Esther 2);

Group 3: Plotting of Haman (see Esther 3—4);
Group 4: Venture of Esther (see Esther 5);
Group 5: Deliverance of the Jews (see Esther 6—10).

• Tell them that they will role-play what happened in their section. They can either have a narrator, they can mime, or they can act out the story with verbal speaking parts. Give the groups ten minutes to put their plays together.

• After all the groups return and act out their portions of Esther, discuss the following:

How was this persecution of the Jews similar to the holocaust?
How was it different?
Why have the Jews been persecuted through the centuries?
How can we as Christians build loving relationships with the Jews in our culture?

OPTION TWO: (FOR A 90-MINUTE SESSION)

Ezra: Public Worship and Confession (15 Minutes)

• Read Ezra 10:1-4 and Nehemiah 8:1-3,5,6 to the whole group. Then divide the group into four smaller ones. Ask them to read Ezra 9—10 and Nehemiah 8—9. Have one person in each small group write down everything the group learns about prayer, worship and learning God's Word in these chapters. After seven minutes, gather the whole group back together.

• Ask one person from each group to report what his or her group has learned. List these things on a chalkboard, flipchart or overhead as the groups report. Then discuss the listed questions with the whole group.

An Overview of Ezra, Nehemiah and Esther

1. The purposes of God may sometimes seem delayed, but they are never abandoned. Judah was in exile but not lost. God was disciplining His people not abandoning them! Through the courage and faith of Mordecai and Esther, God saved His people from extinction (see Esther 1—9).

   Notes:

2. As the book of Ezra opens, Cyrus, king of Persia, makes a proclamation permitting the Jews to return to Jerusalem (see Ezra 1—2).

   Notes:

3. Under the priest Ezra, observing the Law and restoring the Temple sacrifice and worship were established. Though the returning Jews faced many obstacles, they persevered in building the Temple and observing God's law (see Ezra 3—10).

   Notes:

4. God inspired Nehemiah to return to Jerusalem to repair the walls and rebuild the city. Of course, he faced opposition from the Samaritans who had not gone into exile (see Nehemiah 1—13).

   Notes:

CONTINUED

A Prayer of Confession:

Jesus Christ Portrayed in the Old Testament

Genesis portrays Jesus Christ as _____.

Exodus portrays Jesus Christ as _____.

Leviticus portrays Jesus Christ as _____.

Numbers portrays Jesus Christ as _____.

Deuteronomy portrays Jesus Christ as _____.

Joshua portrays Jesus Christ as _____.

Judges portrays Jesus Christ as _____.

Ruth portrays Jesus Christ as _____.

1 and 2 Samuel, Kings and Chronicles all portray Jesus Christ as _____.

Ezra and Nehemiah portray Jesus Christ as _____.

Before next week's session or the start of the next quarter of this study, read:

Sunday: Rejection of Vashti (Esther 1)

Monday: Crowning of Esther (Esther 2)

Tuesday: Plotting of Haman (Esther 3—4)

Wednesday: Venture of Esther (Esther 5)

Thursday: Mordecai Exalted (Esther 6)

Friday: Esther's Feast (Esther 7—8)

Saturday: Deliverance of the Jews (Esther 9—10)

Certificate of Completion

This is to certify that

_____
Name

has completed the course, *What the Bible Is All About 101 Old Testament: Genesis—Esther* on this day

_____

_____
Signed

Bible Study Plans
Leader Instructions

As leader, duplicate the Study Plan pages that follow to distribute to your group. Duplicate the pages in duplex format so they can be easily inserted inside a Bible. Group members have the option of following a one-year plan or a two-year plan.

When you introduce the Study Plan to your group, refer to the information on the "Introduction to Study Chart" page to stimulate interest and communicate the value of this Bible Study Plan. If you have never completed such a plan yourself, join the group in committing to follow through on the monthly readings.

Should much of the current month already be gone, instruct them to simply make the "First Month" on the chart include the rest of this month and next month. Also, if there are any months in the year (e.g., December) when a person knows his or her schedule may not allow time for continuing the study plan, suggest that month be left off the chart and the name of the following month written in its place. During that "vacation" month a person may select one or more favorite sections of Scripture (e.g., Psalms, Proverbs, 1 John) in which to do devotional reading until the schedule is back to normal and the study plan can resume. It is better to plan on taking an extra month or two to complete the study than to get discouraged and quit should reading fall behind.

NOTE: If some people have doubts that they will successfully complete the Bible Study Plan, share a few tips to help them keep going should their determination waver:

1. Tell a friend what you are setting out to do and ask him or her to pray for you and regularly check with you on your progress. Making yourself accountable to someone else will help you maintain your pace and help you apply what you learn.

2. Enlist a friend to join you in the plan. Meeting together regularly to talk and to pray about what you have learned is both beneficial and motivational. Ask God to help you apply one principle you read about each day to your walk with Him.

3. Promise yourself some rewards for completing stages of the plan. You may enjoy anticipating a favorite treat each time you complete a suggested reading goal or all the suggested reading for a month.

Also, think of something special to do at the end of three months or six months or the full year. For example, why not plan a "celebration" to which you will invite a few close friends? Invite them out for dinner or dessert and include a brief explanation of some of the benefits you have gained from your Bible reading and prayer.

4. Pray regularly, telling God your doubts about "sticking it out." Ask Him for help in sticking with the daily readings and for help in understanding how He wants you to apply His Word to your life.

Bible Study Plan Introduction to Study Chart

As valuable as a group study is, there is no substitute for systematic, personal Bible study and prayer to grow in your walk with Christ. The plan outlined here will make Bible reading spiritually enriching as well as help deepen your understanding of the Bible both as the history of God's people and as the remarkable unified Book of God's Plan for all humanity. By following this plan, you can read through the Bible in a year, using the helpful guidance contained in *What the Bible Is All About*.

Some people become discouraged in reading the Bible from beginning to end. Some Old Testament sections are difficult to understand and even more difficult to apply to life today. Therefore, this plan lets you spend time each month in three different sections of the Bible: Old Testament Law and History, Old Testament Poetry and Prophecy, and the New Testament. The monthly Bible passages are of similar length rather than trying to complete a book by an arbitrary date. Thus, some pages in *What the Bible Is All About* are listed as resources in more than one month.

This study plan is flexible, giving you some structure and goals, but allowing you to study in the way that fits you best, perhaps even varying your approach throughout the year. For example:

*   Rather than giving daily assignments that may be burdensome, this plan gives monthly guidelines, letting you set the pace.
*   You may prefer to set aside time every day for Bible study. Or you might enjoy reading in longer time blocks several times a week.
*   You might favor the variety that comes by reading from each of the three main sections at each study session. Or you may elect to complete the month's study of each section separately.
*   You might want to read the recommended sections of *What the Bible Is All About* before starting to read the Bible portions. Or you may choose to read the Bible first, and then use *What the Bible Is All About* to help you understand what you have read.
*   You can decide when to start your study. Keep the chart on the following pages in your Bible or in your copy of *What the Bible Is All About*. As you complete a month's suggested reading, mark the reference on the chart as an indication of your progress.

One-Year
Bible Study Plan

What the Bible Is All About Chart

FIRST MONTH:
Old Testament: Law and History
Genesis 1—37 _____   *WTBIAA* pp. 13-40 _____
Old Testament: Poetry and Prophecy
Job 1—42 _____   *WTBIAA* pp. 173-185 _____
New Testament
Matthew 1—20 _____   *WTBIAA* pp. 337-357 _____

SECOND MONTH:
Old Testament: Law and History
Genesis 38—Exodus 25 _____   *WTBIAA* pp. 40-49 _____
Old Testament: Poetry and Prophecy
Psalm 1—62 _____   *WTBIAA* pp. 187-191 _____
New Testament
Matthew 21—Mark 8 _____   *WTBIAA* pp. 357-371 _____

THIRD MONTH:
Old Testament: Law and History
Exodus 26—Leviticus 23 _____   *WTBIAA* pp. 49-59 _____
Old Testament: Poetry and Prophecy
Psalm 63—117 _____   *WTBIAA* pp. 191-193 _____
New Testament
Mark 9—Luke 6 _____   *WTBIAA* pp. 371-387 _____

FOURTH MONTH:
Old Testament: Law and History
Leviticus 24—Numbers 28 _____   *WTBIAA* pp. 59-71 _____
Old Testament: Poetry and Prophecy
Psalm 118—Proverbs 18 _____   *WTBIAA* pp. 193-199 _____
New Testament
Luke 7—22 _____   *WTBIAA* pp. 387-391 _____

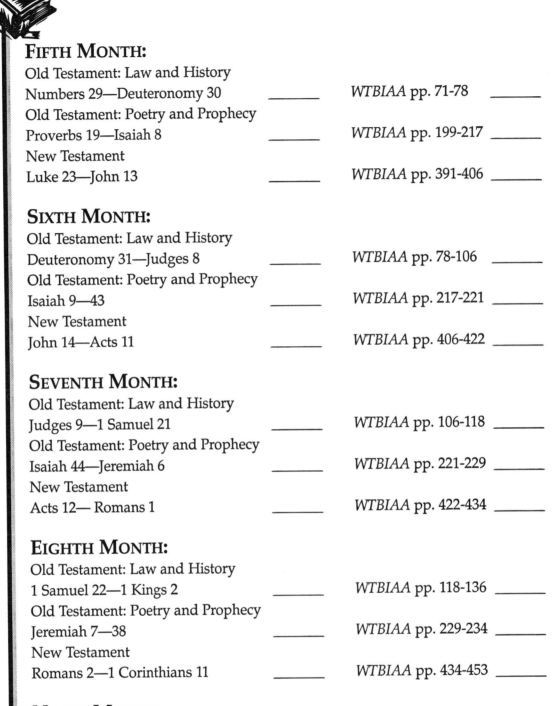

FIFTH MONTH:

Old Testament: Law and History
Numbers 29—Deuteronomy 30 _____ *WTBIAA* pp. 71-78 _____
Old Testament: Poetry and Prophecy
Proverbs 19—Isaiah 8 _____ *WTBIAA* pp. 199-217 _____
New Testament
Luke 23—John 13 _____ *WTBIAA* pp. 391-406 _____

SIXTH MONTH:

Old Testament: Law and History
Deuteronomy 31—Judges 8 _____ *WTBIAA* pp. 78-106 _____
Old Testament: Poetry and Prophecy
Isaiah 9—43 _____ *WTBIAA* pp. 217-221 _____
New Testament
John 14—Acts 11 _____ *WTBIAA* pp. 406-422 _____

SEVENTH MONTH:

Old Testament: Law and History
Judges 9—1 Samuel 21 _____ *WTBIAA* pp. 106-118 _____
Old Testament: Poetry and Prophecy
Isaiah 44—Jeremiah 6 _____ *WTBIAA* pp. 221-229 _____
New Testament
Acts 12— Romans 1 _____ *WTBIAA* pp. 422-434 _____

EIGHTH MONTH:

Old Testament: Law and History
1 Samuel 22—1 Kings 2 _____ *WTBIAA* pp. 118-136 _____
Old Testament: Poetry and Prophecy
Jeremiah 7—38 _____ *WTBIAA* pp. 229-234 _____
New Testament
Romans 2—1 Corinthians 11 _____ *WTBIAA* pp. 434-453 _____

NINTH MONTH:

Old Testament: Law and History
1 Kings 3—2 Kings 10 _____ *WTBIAA* pp. 136-143 _____
Old Testament: Poetry and Prophecy
Jeremiah 39—Ezekiel 15 _____ *WTBIAA* pp. 234-250 _____
New Testament
1 Corinthians 12—Ephesians 6 _____ *WTBIAA* pp. 453-490 _____

TENTH MONTH:

Old Testament: Law and History
2 Kings 11—1 Chronicles 17   _____   *WTBIAA* pp. 143-145   _____
Old Testament: Poetry and Prophecy
Ezekiel 16—45   _____   *WTBIAA* pp. 250-253   _____
New Testament
Philippians 1—Philemon   _____   *WTBIAA* pp. 491-559   _____

ELEVENTH MONTH:

Old Testament: Law and History
1 Chronicles 18—2 Chronicles 31   _____   *WTBIAA* pp. 145-146   _____
Old Testament: Poetry and Prophecy
Ezekiel 46—Amos 9   _____   *WTBIAA* pp. 253-292   _____
New Testament
Hebrews 1—2 Peter 3   _____   *WTBIAA* pp. 561-607   _____

TWELFTH MONTH:

Old Testament: Law and History
2 Chronicles 32—Esther 10   _____   *WTBIAA* pp. 146-171   _____
Old Testament: Poetry and Prophecy
Obadiah 1—Malachi 4   _____   *WTBIAA* pp. 293-334   _____
New Testament
1 John 1—Revelation 22   _____   *WTBIAA* pp. 609-636   _____

Two-Year
Bible Study Plan
What the Bible Is All About Chart

FIRST MONTH:
Old Testament: Law and History
Genesis 1—21 _____ *WTBIAA* pp. 13-40 _____
Old Testament: Poetry and Prophecy
Job 1—20 _____ *WTBIAA* pp. 173-182 _____
New Testament
Matthew 1—11 _____ *WTBIAA* pp. 337-353 _____

SECOND MONTH:
Old Testament: Law and History
Genesis 22—37 _____ *WTBIAA* p. 40 _____
Old Testament: Poetry and Prophecy
Job 21—42 _____ *WTBIAA* pp. 182-185 _____
New Testament
Matthew 12—20 _____ *WTBIAA* pp. 353-357 _____

THIRD MONTH:
Old Testament: Law and History
Genesis 38—Exodus 6 _____ *WTBIAA* pp. 40-45 _____
Old Testament: Poetry and Prophecy
Psalm 1—33 _____ *WTBIAA* pp. 187-189 _____
New Testament
Matthew 21—27 _____ *WTBIAA* pp. 357-360 _____

FOURTH MONTH:
Old Testament: Law and History
Exodus 7—25 _____ *WTBIAA* pp. 45-49 _____
Old Testament: Poetry and Prophecy
Psalm 34—66 _____ *WTBIAA* pp. 189-191 _____
New Testament
Matthew 28—Mark 8 _____ *WTBIAA* pp. 360-376 _____

FIFTH MONTH:

Old Testament: Law and History
Exodus 26—Leviticus 5   _____   *WTBIAA* pp. 49-52   _____
Old Testament: Poetry and Prophecy
Psalm 67—88   _____   *WTBIAA* pp. 191-192   _____
New Testament
Mark 9—16   _____   *WTBIAA* pp. 376-380   _____

SIXTH MONTH:

Old Testament: Law and History
Leviticus 6—23   _____   *WTBIAA* pp. 52-57   _____
Old Testament: Poetry and Prophecy
Psalm 89—117   _____   *WTBIAA* pp. 192-193   _____
New Testament
Luke 1—6   _____   *WTBIAA* pp. 381-387   _____

SEVENTH MONTH:

Old Testament: Law and History
Leviticus 24—Numbers 11   _____   *WTBIAA* pp. 57-65   _____
Old Testament: Poetry and Prophecy
Psalm 118—150   _____   *WTBIAA* pp. 193-194   _____
New Testament
Luke 7—13   _____   *WTBIAA* p. 387   _____

EIGHTH MONTH:

Old Testament: Law and History
Numbers 12—28   _____   *WTBIAA* pp. 65-71   _____
Old Testament: Poetry and Prophecy
Proverbs 1—18   _____   *WTBIAA* pp. 195-199   _____
New Testament
Luke 14—23   _____   *WTBIAA* pp. 387-392   _____

NINTH MONTH:

Old Testament: Law and History
Numbers 29—Deuteronomy 9   _____   *WTBIAA* pp. 71-77   _____
Old Testament: Poetry and Prophecy
Proverbs 19—Ecclesiastes 7   _____   *WTBIAA* pp. 199-202   _____
New Testament
Luke 24—John 6   _____   *WTBIAA* pp. 392-403   _____

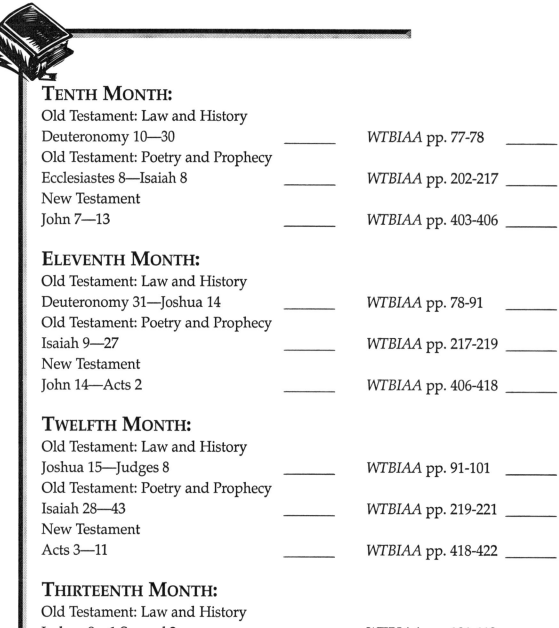

TENTH MONTH:

Old Testament: Law and History
Deuteronomy 10—30 _____ *WTBIAA* pp. 77-78 _____
Old Testament: Poetry and Prophecy
Ecclesiastes 8—Isaiah 8 _____ *WTBIAA* pp. 202-217 _____
New Testament
John 7—13 _____ *WTBIAA* pp. 403-406 _____

ELEVENTH MONTH:

Old Testament: Law and History
Deuteronomy 31—Joshua 14 _____ *WTBIAA* pp. 78-91 _____
Old Testament: Poetry and Prophecy
Isaiah 9—27 _____ *WTBIAA* pp. 217-219 _____
New Testament
John 14—Acts 2 _____ *WTBIAA* pp. 406-418 _____

TWELFTH MONTH:

Old Testament: Law and History
Joshua 15—Judges 8 _____ *WTBIAA* pp. 91-101 _____
Old Testament: Poetry and Prophecy
Isaiah 28—43 _____ *WTBIAA* pp. 219-221 _____
New Testament
Acts 3—11 _____ *WTBIAA* pp. 418-422 _____

THIRTEENTH MONTH:

Old Testament: Law and History
Judges 9—1 Samuel 2 _____ *WTBIAA* pp. 101-112 _____
Old Testament: Poetry and Prophecy
Isaiah 44—59 _____ *WTBIAA* p. 221 _____
New Testament
Acts 12—20 _____ *WTBIAA* pp. 422-425 _____

FOURTEENTH MONTH:

Old Testament: Law and History
1 Samuel 3—21 _____ *WTBIAA* pp. 112-118 _____
Old Testament: Poetry and Prophecy
Isaiah 60—Jeremiah 6 _____ *WTBIAA* pp. 221-229 _____
New Testament
Acts 21—Romans 1 _____ *WTBIAA* pp. 425-434 _____

FIFTEENTH MONTH:

Old Testament: Law and History
1 Samuel 22—2 Samuel 12 _____   *WTBIAA* pp. 118-130 _____
Old Testament: Poetry and Prophecy
Jeremiah 7—23 _____   *WTBIAA* p. 229 _____
New Testament
Romans 2—14 _____   *WTBIAA* pp. 434-442 _____

SIXTEENTH MONTH:

Old Testament: Law and History
2 Samuel 13—1 Kings 2 _____   *WTBIAA* pp. 130-136 _____
Old Testament: Poetry and Prophecy
Jeremiah 24—38 _____   *WTBIAA* pp. 229-234 _____
New Testament
Romans 15—1 Corinthians 11 _____   *WTBIAA* pp. 442-453 _____

SEVENTEENTH MONTH:

Old Testament: Law and History
1 Kings 3—16 _____   *WTBIAA* pp. 136-141 _____
Old Testament: Poetry and Prophecy
Jeremiah 39—52 _____   *WTBIAA* pp. 234-240 _____
New Testament
1 Corinthians 12—2 Cor. 10 _____   *WTBIAA* pp. 453-461 _____

EIGHTEENTH MONTH:

Old Testament: Law and History
1 Kings 17—2 Kings 10 _____   *WTBIAA* pp. 142-143 _____
Old Testament: Poetry and Prophecy
Lamentations 1—Ezekiel 15 _____   *WTBIAA* pp. 240-250 _____
New Testament
2 Corinthians 11—Ephesians 6 _____   *WTBIAA* pp. 461-490 _____

NINETEENTH MONTH:

Old Testament: Law and History
2 Kings 11—1 Chronicles 1 _____   *WTBIAA* pp. 143-145 _____
Old Testament: Poetry and Prophecy
Ezekiel 16—29 _____   *WTBIAA* pp. 250-253 _____
New Testament
Philippians 1—1 Thessalonians 5 _____   *WTBIAA* pp. 491-523 _____

TWENTIETH MONTH:
Old Testament: Law and History
1 Chronicles 2—17 _____ *WTBIAA* pp. 145-146 _____
Old Testament: Poetry and Prophecy
Ezekiel 30—45 _____ *WTBIAA* p. 253 _____
New Testament
2 Thessalonians 1—Philemon _____ *WTBIAA* pp. 525-559 _____

TWENTY-FIRST MONTH:
Old Testament: Law and History
1 Chronicles 18—2 Chronicles 8 _____ *WTBIAA* pp. 145-146 _____
Old Testament: Poetry and Prophecy
Ezekiel 46—Daniel 12 _____ *WTBIAA* pp. 253-272 _____
New Testament
Hebrews 1—13 _____ *WTBIAA* pp. 561-571 _____

TWENTY-SECOND MONTH:
Old Testament: Law and History
2 Chronicles 9—31 _____ *WTBIAA* p. 146 _____
Old Testament: Poetry and Prophecy
Hosea 1—Amos 6 _____ *WTBIAA* pp. 273-290 _____
New Testament
James 1—2 Peter 3 _____ *WTBIAA* pp. 573-607 _____

TWENTY-THIRD MONTH:
Old Testament: Law and History
2 Chronicles 32—Nehemiah 3 _____ *WTBIAA* pp. 146-153 _____
Old Testament: Poetry and Prophecy
Amos 7—Habakkuk 3 _____ *WTBIAA* pp. 290-314 _____
New Testament
1 John 1—Revelation 8 _____ *WTBIAA* pp. 609-628 _____

TWENTY-FOURTH MONTH:
Old Testament: Law and History
Nehemiah 4—Esther 10 _____ *WTBIAA* pp. 153-171 _____
Old Testament: Poetry and Prophecy
Zephaniah 1—Malachi 4 _____ *WTBIAA* pp. 314-334 _____
New Testament
Revelation 9—22 _____ *WTBIAA* pp. 628-636 _____

Teach the Whole Bible at a Fraction of the Price

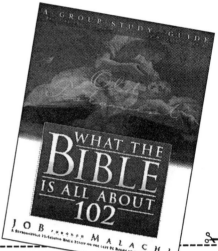

Continue your journey through the Bible and save some money along the way.

Here's a coupon for $2.00 off your purchase of the **What the Bible Is All About 102 Old Testament: Job—Malachi Group Study Guide!** There are 4 books in the entire series, so be on the look-out for your coupon as you begin your New Testament studies next quarter!

You've made it half way through the Old Testament, here's an incentive to help you make it all the way through.

Look for the other volumes of the *What the Bible Is All About 101* series:

**What the Bible Is All About 102
Old Testament:
Job—Malachi Group Study Guide**

**What the Bible Is All About 201
New Testament:
Matthew—Philippians Group Study Guide**

**What the Bible Is All About 202
New Testament:
Colossians—Revelation Group Study Guide**

$2 off

Simply fill out this coupon, sign and return it to your favorite retailer and you'll receive $2 off the purchase price of **What the Bible Is All About 102 Old Testament: Job—Malachi Group Study Guide** (ISBN 08307.17978).

Name_____

Address _____

City _____ State_____ Zip _____

Phone_____

Signature _____
(required for redemption)

Attention consumer: Redeemable only at participating retailers. Not redeemable through Gospel Light. You must pay applicable sales tax. LIMIT ONE COUPON PER CUSTOMER. NOT VALID WITH ANY OTHER OFFERS. Offer available while supplies last. Valid only if signed and phone number included for verification.

Attention Retailer: Customer is eligible for two dollars ($2.00) off the purchase of one copy of **What the Bible Is All About 102 Old Testament: Job—Malachi Group Study Guide** (ISBN 08307.17978) with this coupon, when completed and signed by customer. Please redeem coupon for $2 credit with your next Gospel Light payment: P.O. Box 3875, Ventura, CA 93006-9891. Void where restricted or prohibited. This coupon has no cash value.

Priority Code 1537

Gospel Light

Continue Your Adventure in God's Word

What the Bible Is All About™ is one of the all-time favorite Bible handbooks. This classic 4-million copy best-seller and its family of resources will help you stamp out biblical illiteracy.

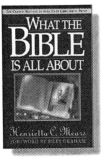

What the Bible Is All About™
Henrietta C. Mears

The classic 4-million-copy-best-seller takes the reader on a personal journey through the entire Bible, covering the basics in a simple, understandable way.

Hardcover • ISBN 08307.16084
Paperback • ISBN 08307.16076

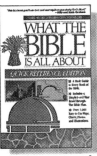

What the Bible Is All About™ Quick-Reference Edition

This easy-to-use Bible handbook gives a brief overview of the people, events and meaning of every book of the Bible. Includes over 1,000 illustrations, charts and time lines.

Hardcover • ISBN 08307.13905
Paperback • ISBN 08307.18486

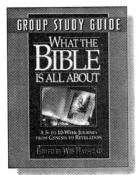

What the Bible Is All About™ Group Study Guide
Wes Haystead

A teaching companion for the best selling classic. In 5 to 10 weeks you will give your students an overview of the Bible with concrete illustrations and clear commentary.
Includes reproducible study sheets.

Group Study Guide • ISBN 08307.16009

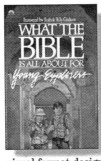

What the Bible Is All About™ for Young Explorers
Frances Blankenbaker

The basics of **What the Bible Is All About,**™ in a graphic visual format designed to make the Bible more approachable for youth.

Hardcover • ISBN 08307.11791
Paperback • ISBN 08307.11627

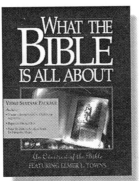

What the Bible Is All About Video Seminar
Elmer L. Towns

Here, in just three hours, Dr. Elmer Towns presents an outline of God's plan for the ages. He shows how this plan is established on six key "turning points" in history. Armed with a clear understanding of these foundation points, students can turn to the Bible with a deeper understanding of its content.

Video Seminar • SPCN 85116.00906
  (Package includes book, reproducible syllabus and 2 video tapes.)
Audio tapes • ISBN 75116.00611

Gospel Light

These resources are available at your local Christian bookstore.

New!

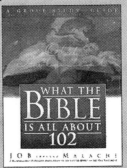
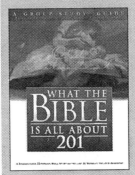
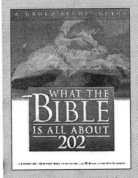